HOW TO BEAT
SIT-&-GO
POKER
TOURNAMENTS

NEIL TIMOTHY

D0036617

I dedicate this book to my parents, family and long-term girl-friend, Ceire, who have always been there for me and supported me no matter what I did. Also, a big thanks to Colm and James who taught me everything I know about poker while we skipped college.

HOW TO BEAT
SIT-&-GO
POKER
TOURNAMENTS

NEIL TIMOTHY

CARDOZA PUBLISHING

Cardoza Publishing is the foremost gaming and gambling publisher in the world with a library of more than 200 up-to-date and easy-to-read books and strategies. These authoritative works are written by the top experts in their fields and with more than 10,000,000 books in print, represent the best-selling and most popular gaming books anywhere.

2011 PRINTING

Copyright © 2007 by Neil Timothy
All Rights Reserved

Library of Congress Catalog Number: 2007941286
ISBN 10: 1-58042-223-3   ISBN 13: 978-1-58042-223-9

Visit our website or write for a full list of Cardoza Publishing books and advanced strategies.

CARDOZA PUBLISHING

P.O. Box 98115, Las Vegas, NV 89193
Toll-Free Phone (800)577-WINS
email: cardozabooks@aol.com
www.cardozabooks.com

About the Author

Neil Timothy is a full time Internet poker player. He decided to drop out of college to play poker as his profession. After a year of playing online poker he found he could make a healthy living by playing sit-and-go poker tournaments and decided to write a book about this subject since, as Neil says, "I found that there was no book covering sit-and-go tournaments in depth. My main objective was to write a book which was easy to understand and read. I found most books covering no-limit hold'em were complex and hard to digest, and for this reason I approached the book in a simplistic way rather than a theoretical one. I believe a basic understanding of the game is critical to becoming a good tournament player."

Table of Contents

1. INTRODUCTION

The strategies and tactics discussed in this book are designed for the lower limit no-limit hold'em sit-and-gos where the buy-ins are less than $50 online or $200 in live games. The players found in these limits are weak, resulting in a lot of dead money up for grabs. When the buy-in goes above these amounts, the standard of play becomes considerably better, though you'll find much of the strategic advice here will still be applicable. You'll also find that the strategies in this book work for the early and middle stages of one-table satellites, which are essentially the same structure (except that there is only one winner as opposed to three).

In the lower-limit games, there is a certain game plan that, if applied correctly, can ensure you make a consistent profit. If you play the way I recommend, you should reach the last six places about 80 percent of the time and get in the money 25 to 35 percent of the time. And that means you'll win money on a consistent basis.

Most of the concepts in this book are solely for sit-and-go tournaments and should not be imported to your cash game simply because many of the plays will not work in standard ring games. This book assumes that you know how to play no-limit hold'em and have a basic understanding of the game, though I have provided a quick primer on the rules.

Following my strategies will improve your sit-and-go game, turning an average player into a good player, and a good player into a bigger winner. You'll learn key concepts and theories you might not know and experience an immediate improvement in your game. I have explained the winning strategies in their simplest forms, while still offering different styles to get you to the winners circle.

You can make money at sit-and-gos on a consistent basis and this book will show you how!

2. WHAT ARE SIT-AND-GOS?

A **sit-and-go (SNG)** is essentially a mini-poker tournament. It is so named because of the fact that you just sit down and the tournament starts as soon as the table is full. Each player at the table pays an identical fee to enter the tournament and receives an identical amount of chips. Unlike cash games, where you can stick your hand back into your pocket and buy more chips, you have to make do with what you are given making your chips more valuable to you.

The fee to enter makes up the prize pool and is normally distributed as follows:

> 1st place receives 50 percent
>
> 2nd place receives 30 percent
>
> 3rd place receives 20 percent

After a predetermined period of time, the blinds increase, forcing the tournament to have a winner relatively quickly. Some sites offer six- or nine-player tournaments, but the standard sit-and-gos have ten players. Obviously the fewer the number of players, the less money there is for the prize poll. For this reason, I recommend sticking to the ten-man tables.

Sit-and-gos are getting more and more popular among poker players. I personally like sit-and-gos because you know roughly how long one will last—about an hour to an hour and a half online and up to two hours or so live—and you are only risking a small amount of your money. During this period of time you can experience playing at a full table, a short-handed table, and heads-up if you are lucky. This is priceless experience for any serious poker player who wants to improve different aspects of his game.

All this experience will pay dividends if you ever get to the final table of a multitable tournament. These final tables are difficult to reach, making it hard to know what to do when you are there. But if you play sit-and-gos regularly, you will have a massive advantage over your opponents with the knowledge you have gained.

Sit-and-gos are usually hold'em games played as no-limit—there is no maximum amount that can be bet. During any hand, you can bet your entire stack of chips, which means that your tournament life is always in jeopardy. The flip side is that you can win all your opponents chips at any time. The excitement and extreme tension of the all-in bet is one of the reasons no-limit tournaments have became so popular. Throughout the book, I will address how and what to bet in the right situations, giving you a better feel for the game so that you will be the one winning all the chips.

3. HOLD'EM BASICS

In no-limit hold'em, two cards are dealt face down to each player and a round of betting takes place. This round is called the **preflop**. When the first round of betting is complete, three communal cards, called the **flop**, are turned face up in the center of the table. That is followed by a fourth community card and another round of betting, called the **turn**. Then the fifth and final community card is turned over. This is called the **river**. This will be the last round of betting for the hand.

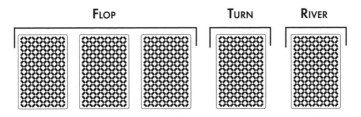

Upon conclusion of all betting on the river, the remaining players show their cards. This is the **showdown**. The best five-card hand using a combination of a player's two private cards and the five communal cards is the winner. If two or more players have identically ranked hands, the winners split the pot.

THE BUTTON AND THE BLINDS

Before each deal, the two players to the left of the **button**, the marker that rotates around the table and indicates the player who occupies the dealer's position, are required to post the blinds. The **blinds** are forced bets that get immediate money into the pot and give players something to go after. The player to the immediate left of the dealer is the **small blind**, and the player to his left is the **big blind**. The big blind is typically twice the amount of the small blind.

STRUCTURE OF SIT-AND-GOS

During each tournament there are blind levels, which increase in size (normally double) after a set time or number of hands. The increased pressure of the blind bets forces players to risk their chips to survive, leading to players busting out and the tournament's end when one player has accumulated all the chips in play.

BETTING BASICS

Preflop, players can either call or raise the blind bet, or they most fold their hand. On this and the following rounds, if there is no bet, players may check or bet. If there is a bet, players may either call, raise, reraise (if another player has raised)—or they must fold.

4. POSITION

Position, where you sit relative to the button, is one of the most important aspects of Texas hold'em and should always be taken into account when deciding whether to play a hand and how to play it. It is vital to know how to play from the different positions found at a full table.

Below is a table found in the early stages of a tournament. It has been divided into four sections to show you the best and worst positions to play from. In this illustration, the button is in the 8 seat.

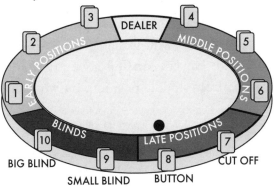

SEATS 1, 2 AND 3

The three seats to the left of the big blind are the **early positions** found at a full table.* Only premium hands should be played from here. With a lot of players acting after you, there is a good chance that if you play a mediocre hand, you will run into a better one. Normally when players raise from here you have to give them respect for a good hand.

In most tournaments or ring games you have to mix up your play and occasionally raise from these positions with mediocre hands to stop your opponents from getting a read on you. But since sit-and-go tournaments are so fast and you will rarely be playing with the same players, there is no need to vary your play from the different positions.

SEATS 4, 5 AND 6

These seats are the **middle positions** found at a full table. More mediocre hands can be played from here since there are fewer hands acting after you than in early position, giving you less chance of running into a bigger hand. Players can still have premium hands when raising from middle position, but you should re-

---

* Note that I have chosen to designate early, middle and late positions after the big blind position (and not including the blinds in early position, as is conventional), and to separate out the discussion for the two blinds positions (seats 9 and 10), because strategy in sit-and-go tournaments must be treated much differently than in other form of poker. Keep that in mind for the positional discussions throughout this book.

spect a raise from early position more than from middle position. The higher the number on the seat the more likely your opponent's hand is mediocre; for example, a raise from seat 6 would be less intimidating than a raise from seat 4.

SEATS 7 AND 8 (THE CUTOFF AND THE BUTTON)

These **late positions**—the **cutoff seat** (the seat to the right of the button) and the button—are the best seats to play hands from because of the advantage you gain on every betting round as a result of seeing what your opponents do before the flop, on the flop, and so on. These are also great positions to steal the blinds from since few players act after you. However, since stealing blinds is not important in the early stages of a sit-and-go, all you need to know for now is that your starting hand requirements when playing from late position can loosen up considerably compared to early position.

SEATS 9 AND 10 (THE BLINDS)

The blinds are problem positions for many novice players. Playing hands from the blinds incorrectly leads to a lot of trouble in sit-and-go tournaments. Although you are still able to see what everyone does preflop, you are at a big disadvantage on the flop and after, having to act first on every betting round. Playing from the blinds is a complex matter, so I have dedicated a chapter, "Playing from the Blinds," to it later in the book.

5. EARLY STAGE HAND SELECTION

Now that you have learned the different positions found at a table, you need to know the different hands you should play from each position. This will help you know what to do depending on your hand and position.

When it is your turn to act, a number of factors will influence the way you play it or even if you should play your hand at all. Not every scenario or situation that will occur can be covered, but I will give you enough guidelines on how to play certain hands in the early stages of a tournament to be ready for most situations.

A-A

PREFLOP

Aces is the best possible hand preflop, but it can get you in trouble if the hand is not played correctly. Until something comes along to improve your aces, it is *only* one pair, so you want to protect it by raising. Raising will give your hand a greater chance of holding up by stopping your opponents from seeing the flop cheaply with weak hands. The more players there are in the pot, the more chances your hand has of being beaten. The other advantage of raising is that when you do get called, it will build the size of the pot.

You should raise with aces from any position and, if there is already a raise on the table, you should reraise three times what your opponent put in for the raise. For example, if your opponent opens for $60 (four times the big blind) in early position, you should now reraise to $180.

ON THE FLOP

Ideally, when you do raise, you want just one caller on the flop, two at the most. If the flop comes with a couple of **picture cards** (jacks, queens and kings), I recommend betting since your opponent could have easily made a second-best hand that he'll find worth calling. Even if the flop is checked to you, I still recommend betting since there is a good chance your opponent could have a hand. Giving **free cards**, cards a player gets without having to pay anything for them, can be costly when you only have a pair. If one of your opponents has already bet, don't be scared to reraise, especially if there is a picture card on the board.

If there were three or more callers preflop and you are **check-raised** (an opponent checks and then raises after you bet), you have to consider folding since most players who check-raise have made at least two pair or a set. However, if the flop comes with a picture card, don't be afraid to stick it all in since a lot of the time your opponents will check-raise with just **top pair** (a pocket card that forms a pair with the highest card on board). Due to the small amount of chips you receive in a sit-and-go, you sometimes have to go with your hand. When you raise preflop and then bet the flop, you are committing a lot of chips to the hand, so you can't afford to be second-guessing yourself. This may sometimes lead to an early exit, but more often than not you will have the best of it.

K-K

PREFLOP
Kings should be played the same way as aces preflop. If there are any all ins, you should call as the chances of you being up against aces are slim.

ON THE FLOP
You should play kings the same way as aces on the flop, the only difference being that if an ace comes and a bet is made you should, in general, let go of your hand, especially when the pot is multiway. Most players who call a raise preflop will be holding an ace in

their hand, particularly in the lower-limit tournaments where players will call raises with any **rag ace**—an ace with a weak side card.

However, if it is checked to you on an ace-high flop, that's a different story. Now you should come out betting. If your opponents don't have an ace in their hand, they will be just as scared of the ace as you are. In fact, they should be even more scared of it because you have represented an ace in your hand with your preflop raise. If the pot is multiway, I wouldn't recommend betting out since there is a good chance someone is trying to check-raise you. Just check and see what happens on the turn. If they all check again then you should make a bet.

Q-Q

PREFLOP

The same rules apply when raising with queens as with aces and kings. If you are reraised all in, you should still call. The chances of being up against aces or kings is still slim. Keep in mind that the standard of play can be poor in the lower-limit tournaments. I've seen players push all in with rag aces or **suited connectors,** cards in sequential order and of the same suit, so you can't afford to fold queens preflop against an all-in raise.

If, however, there are two or more all ins, calling is out of the question as there is now a good chance you are dominated or at best an approximate 50-50 against an opponent's A-K—plus you have another player's hand to beat as well. It is too early in the tournament to be taking coin tosses like that.

ON THE FLOP

If the flop comes with no **overcards**, a card on board that is higher than the pair you hold, you should bet to stop opponents with overcards from chasing an ace or a king on the turn or river. If an ace and a king come on the flop, you should usually fold to any serious betting, especially if the pot is multiway. If you are in the hand heads-up and only one overcard comes, don't be afraid to bet. Your opponent will only connect with the flop one in three times, so most of the time you will be holding the winning hand. If you are reraised or called, you should, in general, fold and cut your losses or try and check it down to the river.

J-J

PREFLOP

Jacks can be a problem hand in the early stages of a sit-and-go tournament. The way you play them depends on your position. If you are in early position, you should limp into the pot. This will keep the pot small but also make the hand easier to get away from if the flop comes scary. If someone raises behind you, you should call and see what happens on the flop.

When you receive jacks in middle or late position, you should raise with them, especially if there have been **limpers**, players who call (as opposed to raise). You want to try and pick up the pot there and then. If there has been a raise from early position, you should call with the intention of playing your position on the flop. However, when the raise comes from middle or late position, I recommend reraising to find out where you are in the hand. If your opponents reraise or move all in, you know you are behind and can fold. That's the trick with jacks in the early stages of the tournament. Either you play them cheaply or protect them with a raise and define your hand.

If there are any all ins you should fold unless you know the player to be a loose **maniac**, a player who bets and raises recklessly. Most players who move all in will be holding at least A-Q or higher, giving you about a 50-50 shot or making you a massive **dog** (longshot) if you're going up against aces, kings or queens.

ON THE FLOP
If you limped in with the jacks preflop, you will have to play them carefully, especially if the pot has become multiway. Don't get carried away with your pair if an overcard comes on the flop. In an unraised multiway

pot, it is impossible to put your opponents on hands since they could have limped with anything. When you limp with your jacks, you are trying to hit a **set** (a three-of-a-kind hand) on the flop and win a massive pot. If you don't make your set you have to make a decision as to whether or not to play the hand any further. Not playing prudently can lead to a lot of early exits. When you do make a set and the board comes with an overcard, I strongly recommend betting since there is a good chance somebody else has made a second-best hand and will commit all his chips.

If you were the raiser in the hand and got called by a limper or someone in a later position, you should come out betting when the flop comes with no overcards. This will prevent your opponent from outdrawing you on the turn.

Whenever the flop is checked to you and you have been the aggressor preflop, you should come out betting almost every time. You should do so even if there is an overcard to your jacks present, since again, there's a good chance your opponent has nothing and you can pick up the pot there and then. If you are **played back at**, that is, when your opponent raises after you bet or raise, you will have to give your opponent credit for a hand.

The lower limit sit-and-gos are full of tight, weak players who will usually fold when you bet into them.

(**Tight players** play only premium cards and thus few hands.) If they do play back at you it normally means they have a hand. Of course, they could just be bluffing. Either way you can't justify carrying on in the hand. That's the thing with poker—even if you are the best player in the world, sometimes you have to fold the winning hand.

A-K AND A-Q

PREFLOP

These hands can pose problems in sit-and-gos and a lot of inexperienced players play them incorrectly. The most common mistake made in the early stages of a sit-and-go tournament is raising too big with these hands. Overbetting the pot preflop will only lead to you being called when you are beaten.

Let me show you what I mean by overbetting.

EXAMPLE

You have $1,000, the blinds are $15/$30, and you raise $400, committing yourself to the hand. No one in his right mind is going to call your raise unless he is holding aces, kings, queens, jacks or A-K. There is no point in overbetting the pot when the only time you will get called is when you are a massive underdog or, at best, have a hand equal to your opponents.

The correct way to play A-K is to raise four times the big blind. If you are reraised you can fold and live to fight another day. If somebody has already raised the pot you should flat call. Again, this will keep the pot small and give you the advantage of position on the flop. When there have been limpers you should still raise to try and pick up the pot there and then. If there has been a raise followed by reraises you will have to fold as you are either dominated by aces or kings or at best about a 50-50 shot against queens or jacks. It is not worth getting involved in the hand if you have nothing serious invested in the pot.

Whenever you raise with A-K you are just trying to win the pot preflop, so when there's been an all in and a call, A-K loses all its fold equity (discussed in "The Bubble" chapter), turning it into a very average hand.

It's not until the middle and later stages of the tournament that A-K comes into its own. During these stages the blinds will become high and there will be a lot of big pots preflop. In these cases, when there's a raise, you can come over the top of the raiser, giving you two ways of winning the pot—either by making the raiser fold, or if you are called, winning the showdown. You don't want any of these confrontations in the early stages of the tournament so play your A-K with caution.

A-Q is played exactly the same as A-K with one exception—if there has been a raise from an early position you should fold. This stops the risk of you running into A-K and being severely dominated.

ON THE FLOP

A-K and A-Q are played exactly the same way on the flop. When you raise preflop, the way you will play the hand depends on how many players call your raise. In general, the more players that there are in the pot, the more inclined you should be to bluff. If you did manage to get the hand heads-up you will have to play it aggressively. Even if you haven't connected with the flop, with the small amount of chips you are given in sit-and-gos, you can't afford to raise preflop and then just check the flop. Checking will give your opponent the perfect opportunity to bluff you off the hand.

Two-thirds of the time you won't connect with the flop so you will have to keep the aggression up by making a **continuation bet** (betting the flop after raising preflop). If you are called, you should **shut down**—discontinue betting—as you don't want to commit any more chips to the hand.

If you do connect with the flop you should come out betting. You don't want to get tricky with top pair. In the early stages of the tournament you are just trying to survive, so playing straightforward poker will stop you from being outdrawn and busting out.

POCKET PAIRS TENS AND LOWER

PREFLOP

Pocket pairs should only be played when you are in a good position with three or more players already in the pot. You want to see the flop as cheaply as possible, trying to hit a set and winning big pots. If there has been a big raise you should fold. That's why you need position when limping. You don't want to call from early position and then get raised by someone behind you. Pocket pairs should be played rarely and only under the correct circumstances.

ON THE FLOP

Pocket pairs play easy on the flop. If you don't make your set you should fold to any betting, even if you have an overpair to the flop. You shouldn't get carried away with small and meduim pocket pairs. You don't know what type of hand your opponent could have made in an unraised multiway pot. For example, someone with a higher pair could even have limped in. If it is checked around to you, don't bet. Take a free card and try to make your set on the turn.

When you do make your set, you can either **slowplay** it—play a big hand weakly to encourage a bluff or to let an opponent make a hand that will be second-best—or play it aggressively, depending on what you feel will win the most chips off your opponent. If the flop includes picture cards I recommend betting since chances are someone has made a second-best hand. Playing sets aggressively will sometimes stop your opponents getting away from their hands, whereas check-raising can give the strength of your hand away.

SUITED CONNECTORS

PREFLOP

The main decision as to whether or not you should play suited connectors in a sit-and-go tournament is the amount of chips you start off with. If you are given $1,500 or more, you can play suited connectors in the early stages of the tournament, because with more chips you can chase flushes and straights on the flop without having to worry about being left short-stacked if you don't make your draw. If you have less than this amount of chips, I wouldn't recommend playing suited connectors as it can get expensive. With such a small amount of chips you're looking to use them when you have the best of it, not wasting them on draws. If you have enough chips to gamble with, $1,500 or more, you should play suited connectors the same way as pocket pairs preflop.

ON THE FLOP

If you do catch a small flush or straight on the flop you should bet big to stop someone else from catching a bigger flush or higher straight on the turn. The more players in the pot, the higher the chance there is that one of them will have a high picture card in the same suit or a high straight draw. Betting out will make it expensive for your opponents to see the turn.

The chances of you flopping a flush or straight are around 118 to 1, so more often than not you will be flopping draws. When you are one card away from your straight or flush you have to make a decision on whether or not to chase the draw. For your decision to be correct you need to get the correct odds from the pot. If you have four parts of a flush after the flop, you will make it one out of three times (2 to 1) by the river. Therefore, for your call to be correct, the pot has to offer you odds of 2 to 1 or higher. That is, for every $1 it costs you to bet, there needs to be $2 already in the pot. The following example shows you how to calculate pot odds.

EXAMPLE

The pot contains $500, your opponent bets $100 and everyone folds to you. To calculate your pot odds you add your opponent's bet to the pot (in this case, $500 plus $100 equals $600), then see how much it is to call. Since it's $100 to call, you are getting 6 to 1 odds on your bet, giving you the correct odds to make the play.

If you only chase draws with the correct odds you will be making the right decisions over the long run.

When you have a draw I don't recommend **semibluffing** (betting with a drawing hand that is likely second-best at the moment, but could improve to be the best), even in late position. You will be in multi-way pots so there's a good chance your semibluff won't succeed and you may even get check-raised. If one of your opponents is trapping with a hand, you want to punish him for not charging you to see the turn, so check and see if you can make your draw for free. If you do complete your flush or straight on the turn you should play it aggressively to stop anyone outdrawing you on the river.

The main strategy for a sit-and-go is to play tight poker in the early stages of the tournament and loose-aggressive towards the later stages. With this strategy, the only hands you should play in the early stages of a tournament are the ones described in this chapter. Towards the later stages of a tournament, when the game becomes short-handed, all these hands become massive.

Trouble hands like A-J, A-10, K-Q, K-J, K-10, etc. shouldn't be played in the early stages of the tournament because you don't know where you are in the hand. If you raise and are called, you can get yourself in a lot of trouble, especially if you connect on the flop.

Throughout this book, I will make a lot of generalizations on what to do in various situations and how to play certain hands. However, don't be afraid to play outside these guidelines. Every hand should be played taking into consideration your opponents' playing styles and tendencies. For instance, I said to fold queens against two all in raises. But if you have seen two players push all in a few times and it happens again, don't be afraid to call. You must adjust for particular circumstances and not be scared to make a mistake—this will help you get a better feel for the game.

However, towards the later stages of a tournament when the game has become short-handed, all these trouble hands go up in value as there are fewer hands out there to beat you. There is less chance you will be dominated or **outkicked** (a hand where the highest pocket card is equal to an opponent's, but the secondary card is lesser in rank) when you get action. I call all these trouble hands "stealing hands," and have dedicated a chapter to them later in the book.

6. STRATEGY

Your game plan will change for the different stages of the tournament. Below are the different strategies for these stages.

EARLY STAGE STRATEGY (BLIND LEVELS 1 TO 3)

The main factor that affects your strategy when playing a sit-and-go is the blinds in relation to your stack size. During the early stages of the tournament when the blinds are small you should employ a premium hand strategy. You'll fold 75 to 80 percent of your hands preflop and only play the premium hands described in the previous chapter.

When you get involved in a hand you shouldn't be making any fancy plays or bluffs; just play solid tight poker. Playing loose or making bluffs can result in you losing valuable chips. These chips are more important than you may think.

EXAMPLE

You start off with $1,000 in chips and you waste $350 by bluffing or playing loose. You are now left with $650, already putting yourself at a disadvantage for the later stages of the tournament. If you double up now you will only have $1,300 in chips, just $300 more than what you started off with. But if you had played tight and lost $150 through the blinds you would still have $850. Now if you double up you will have $1,700, $700 more than what you started off with. So when you lose $350 in the early stages of the tournament you actually have lost $700 because of the double-up value those chips have.

Instead of getting involved in a lot of hands you should concentrate on the players at the table. This is the best time in the tournament to observe the different types of players you are up against. Any information you can gain will help you for the later stages of the tourna-ment when you start to play more hands against them. Normally, there will be two to three players knocked out in the early stages of a tournament due to bad play or premium hands meeting premium hands, so just playing tight will get you into the last six almost every time.

MIDDLE STAGE STRATEGY (BLIND LEVELS 4 TO 6)

During the middle stage of a tournament, you should still play tight poker, but your aggression should go up a level. Hands like A-J, K-Q, K-J and A-10 are all now playable in good position. The main factor that should influence your hand selection is the number of players left at this stage of the tournament. The fewer players left, the lower your standard of hand selection should be. If there are nine or ten players left, then you can't raise from early position with mediocre hands as you run a higher risk of running into a bigger hand.

You want to pay close attention to everyone's stack size in relation to the blinds and be conscious of when the next level is approaching. The blinds will get bigger at this stage of the tournament, giving you a great opportunity to see whose blinds you can and cannot steal. Watch for players who give up their blinds to raises or are not making up their small blind when it hasn't been raised. These are signs of a tight player who can be taken advantage of in the later stages of the tournament.

LATE STAGE STRATEGY (BLIND LEVELS 6 TO MAX)

In the late stages of a sit-and go tournament there will normally be six or fewer players remaining, so you should change gears and become more aggressive in your play. The bigger blinds mean there are bigger pots before anyone has even played a hand, so aggressive play is rewarded. Blind stealing now becomes a big part of your game plan. Before we go into hand selection and strategies, you will have to learn the different positions found in the latter stages.

7. SHORT-HANDED PLAY

In this chapter, I will discuss how short-handed games (six or fewer players) should be played differently from full-table games. Position is the main factor in short-handed play and will dictate whether or not you should play a hand. In early position, you don't know what your opponents might have or what they are going to do, making your mediocre hands vulnerable. But when you are in late position you get to see what everyone else does, giving you an advantage over your opponents.

In general you should play more hands aggressively in better position and fewer hands in bad position. For example, raise with J-10 on the button but not when you are first to act.

Below is an illustration of a short-handed table with the different positions you will play from.

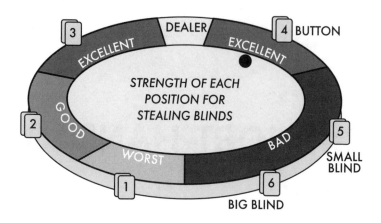

SEAT 1

This seat is the worst position to try and steal the blinds from. I would only recommend trying to steal from here when you have a big stack, or are short-stacked and need to push just to survive the next orbit of blinds.

SEAT 2

This is a good position for stealing the blinds when the game is tight or if you have a big stack. I wouldn't recommend any steals from here if you are average- or short-stacked, as again, a lot of the time you will run into a hand and end up short-stacked or out of the tournament.

SEATS 3 AND 4

These are excellent positions to steal the blinds from because of the advantage you will have on all the betting rounds if you are called. More importantly, the chances of your steal being successful become significantly higher because of the small number of players acting after you.

SEATS 5 AND 6

These are bad positions to call raises from. When playing from these positions I recommend two options—reraising or folding. Calling will put you at a massive disadvantage on the flop when you have to act first. When reraising, you need a good feel for what your opponent might have. If the raises come from seat 3 or 4 then there's a good chance they might just be stealing, but a raise from seat 1 or 2 should be respected.

It is also worth noting that seat 5 (the small blind) is an excellent position to steal the big blind from if no one else has entered the pot, as the chances of the big blind finding a hand are slim.

It's important that you never limp from any of the positions described above. At this stage of the tournament the blinds are a high portion of your stack, so you are either raising or folding when playing a hand.

Now that you know how to play from the different positions found at a short-handed game you will have to learn the different hands you should start to play. In a short-handed game there are fewer cards out there, so there is less chance of any player holding a premium hand. Because of this, you should open up your hand selection.

STEALING HANDS

I have divided the hands you should now play into two groups. I call these hands, **stealing hands**. Except for the premium starting hands listed in Group 1, these are hands that you would not normally play aggressively in the early stages of a sit-and go. However, because the game has become short-handed, they should be played aggressively preflop to try to force out opponents and steal the blinds.

STEALING HANDS GROUP 1

All the hands described below are big hands when the game becomes short-handed and should be played aggressively from any position. They are good to reraise or call an all in with.

A-A

K-K

Q-Q

J-J

10-10

9-9

A-K

A-Q

A-J

If you have A-J, tens, or nines, call all-in raises only if they come from a short stack and will not cost you more than half your stack if you lose.

STEALING HANDS GROUP 2

Group 2 stealing hands are okay to raise or move all in with in good position, but not to reraise or call all ins with.

Any pair

Any ace

K-Q

K-J

K-10

Q-J

J-10 suited

10-9 suited

9-8 suited

The purpose of playing the Group 2 hands is to help you accumulate chips by stealing the blinds. You don't want any confrontations with these hands. If you are reraised or someone else has already raised, you should fold.

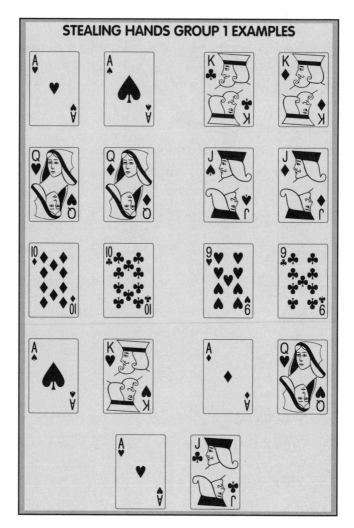

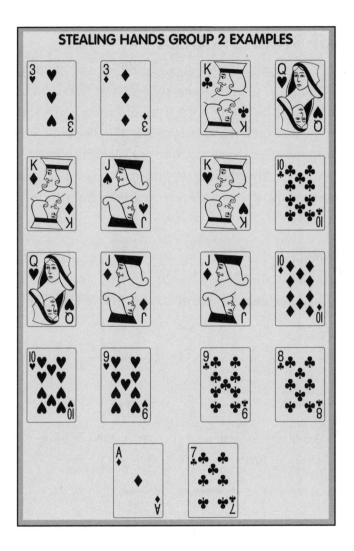

STEALING HANDS GROUP 2 EXAMPLES

LATE STAGE STRATEGY

During the later stages of a sit-and-go, the blinds become high in relation to everyone's stacks. This means there won't be many flops seen and near perfect pre-flop poker will have to be played. The high blinds result in mistakes being severely punished. You can turn this to your advantage by getting tricky with big hands. Slowplaying or check-raising well reap rewards in the later stages.

EXAMPLE

The blinds are $150/$300. It's limped around to the button who has $2,000 in chips. He raises to $600 with

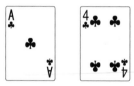

The small blind folds and you are in the big blind with $3,000. You have

Instead of reraising like you usually would, you can get tricky and call.

The flop comes

Instead of raising and letting your opponent get away from his hand, you can go for a check-raise. Your opponent is going to think you have nothing with a flop like that. The pot is now $1,350 and the only way your opponent can win the hand is with a bluff. With only $1,250 in chips left, he will have to move all in, leaving you with an easy call.

The obvious disadvantage to this play is that an ace could come on the flop, putting your kings in a vulnerable position, while if you had moved all in preflop, your opponents might have folded. There is always a risk in slowplaying big hands in the latter stages of a tournament, but this strategy will get the maximum value from them.

You have to adjust your strategy based on the size of your stack in relation to the blinds. This is the single most important factor that affects the way you play.

IDENTIFYING YOUR STACK SIZE

Towards the latter stages of the tournament you will need to know what the average stack is in order to make the correct strategy decisions. The average stack is easy to find; all you have to do is divide the total number of chips the table started with by the number of players that are left. So, in a ten-player sit-and-go where every player started with $1,500 in chips, there would be $15,000 of chips in play. If five players remain, the average stack size would be $3,000; if four players, a bit under $4,000 ($3,750); if three players, the average stack size would be $5,000.

Online, it is easy to know the exact stack sizes because they are displayed right in front of each player. The average stack size is easy to find as well on all online sites. Go to the tournament lobby, where it will be displayed In live, land-based games, visually, you can get a pretty good idea how your opponents stack up.

Stack sizes would be classified as below.

Average Stack	About the average number of chips
Short Stack	About half the average stack size or less
Big Stack	About one and half times the average stack

For example, if you're on the bubble (four players remaining) and have about $3,500-$4,000 in chips, you're average-stacked. To make the math easy, let's say the average stack size is $4,000. A big stack would be around $6,000, while a short stack would be about $2,000 or less.

To classify stack sizes so that you can make the right decisions, you only need to know *approximate* amounts. For the purposes of strategy, when five players are left, a stack with $5,500 is just as much a big stack as one with $6,000 (just with a bit less room to maneuver).

EXAMPLE

There are four players left and $15,000 of chips are in play. The average stack size is about $4,000 ($3,750). Player One has $7,700, Player Two has $3,700, Player Three has $2,100 in chips and Player Four has $1,500. Player One is considered big-stacked, Player Two average-stacked, and Players Three and Four are short-stacked.

PLAYING THE SHORT STACK

The only reason you should be short-stacked at this stage of the tournament is if one of your premium hands didn't hold up. If this has happened you should tighten up your play. The fewer chips you have, the more precious they are to you. That's the major difference between cash games and tournaments. In a cash game you can put your hand back in your pocket and rebuy, whereas in tournaments, your chips can never be replaced. Try to hang on as long as you can and pick a good situation to push with a stealing hand.

The key consideration for when you should move all in is if you can be the first one into the pot. This way you have two ways of winning the hand—either by making everyone fold preflop, or getting called and winning the showdown. If you are selectively aggressive, with a bit of luck you can get yourself back in the game. Never give up! You are only one double up away from becoming average-stacked again.

PLAYING THE AVERAGE STACK

If you employ the strategy described in this book you will find yourself average-stacked most of the time in the latter stages. Playing with an average stack is one of the hardest things to do in no-limit hold'em tournaments. You don't really have enough chips to bully the other players, but you also can't sit back and let yourself be **blinded out** (losing most or all of your chips to erosion from the blinds without playing hands). If you receive any of the stealing hands in good position, try to pick up the blinds with them. The key to stealing blinds is to do it while you still have some chips to play around with. This way you won't get yourself in trouble if you are played back at, since you can still afford to fold.

It is in these situations, when you are stealing, that your observation of the other players will pay off. You want to steal against the tight, average stacks left at the table. Your raise will have a higher chance of success against them than a short-stacked player in one of the blind positions who may feel committed to his hand. With one double up, short stacks become average-stacked and you will be short-stacked. Also, try and stay away from the big-stacked blinds unless you have a premium hand, since they are the players at the table who can afford to gamble with you.

Survival is still your main priority at this stage of the tournament. If you are overaggressive, you could run into a big hand and end up out of the tournament. You can't win the tournament here but you can lose it.

PLAYING THE BIG STACK

If you have a big stack at this stage of the tournament, you have either doubled up earlier with a premium hand or got lucky. Now that you have more chips, you can afford to be more creative and adventurous with your play. It's your job to bully the average and short stacks at the table, putting the pressure on their blinds at every opportunity. You should raise with all the stealing hands from any position since you can now afford to be involved in a few pots.

The only time you should tighten up is when there is another big stack acting after you. The last thing you want is to be going heads-up with a mediocre hand against the only player at the table who can end your tournament. Sometimes you will find another big stack at the table who got his stack by playing too many hands and calling too much. It's important that you recognize this type of player as early as possible and stay away from any confrontations with him.

8. THE BUBBLE

A tournament is said to be on the **bubble** when it is one place away from the money. In a ten man sit-and-go, the last three players get paid, so when there are four players left, it's the bubble stage of the tournament. The bubble is the most important part of any tournament because all your hard work can mean nothing if you go out here. Every decision now is critical as the blinds are usually a big portion of everyone's stack. One mistake will lead to you being short-stacked or out of the tournament.

Before you decide to play a hand, you have to learn the different positions found around a four-handed table. Below is an illustration of the bubble with some guidelines on how to play this stage of a sit-and-go tournament.

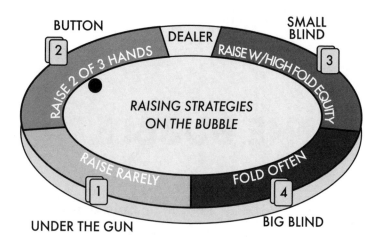

SEAT 1 (UNDER THE GUN)

Being **under the gun** means you are the first player to act in a betting round. In other words, you are to the immediate left of the big blind on the preflop. This is the seat from which you should be the least aggressive. You can raise with stealing hands under the gun but don't try to make a move with complete rubbish. You want to keep raising to a minimum from here, especially if you are average-stacked. Wait for a better position to get your money in. The main benefit of folding from this position is that it gives the three other players at the table a chance to battle it out. The only time you can confidently raise from under the gun is if you are big-stacked and your opponents are all short-stacked or passive medium stacks.

SEAT 2 (THE BUTTON)

When you are big-stacked, the button becomes a powerful position. You should raise about two-thirds of your hands from the button. This aggression will help you build a bigger chip lead over your opponents.

The only time you should be wary when playing from the button is when Seat One has limped in or raised. He has either limped with a premium hand to trap your aggressive style or raised with rubbish. Either way, you don't know and he will probably be **pot-committed** (having half or more of one's chips invested in the pot so that a player is committed to putting the rest in if raised) due to the high blinds, so only your strongest hands should be played when seat one has entered the pot.

SEAT 3 (SMALL BLIND)

When no one else has entered the pot, the small blind has a great opportunity to steal the big blind. The main factor that will influence whether or not you should raise is how much fold equity your raise will have. If you are short-stacked and there is a loose big stack in the blind, you obviously don't have much fold equity.

Ideally, you want to be the big stack raising a medium or short stack's big blind. When you raise as a big stack, I recommend putting in the exact amount of your opponent's chips. This stops your opponent from having the option of reraising and pushing you off the hand. You will also gain a psychological edge over your opponent by putting his tournament life on the line, not yours.

The main benefit of making an all-in move is that you have the ability to make a player throw away a winning hand. For example, you move all in from the small blind with K-4 and the big blind folds K-5. If somebody has already limped from another position don't call from the small blind position with mediocre hands like you would in the early stages of the tournament. Either fold or raise. The high blinds mean even half bets can be expensive.

SEAT 4 (BIG BLIND)

We know the big blind can be a hard position to play from. If you are medium- or short-stacked and the pot is raised, you should fold nearly all your hands from here. If there has been a limper from under the gun or on the button, alarm bells should go off, especially if the limper is usually aggressive. There is a good chance the limper is trying to trap you with a premium hand.

The key to playing the big blind position is to not call many hands. Remember, you are not going to connect with the flop two-thirds of the time. So if you do call, you will be checking the majority of the time, giving your opponent the perfect opportunity to bluff you.

STACK SIZE

Once you know the different positions, you need to know the strategies for the bubble. Your stack size will dictate the way you play.

SHORT STACK

When you find yourself short-stacked on the bubble, you will have to double up or hang on by stealing a couple of blinds. There is a skill to playing a short stack and although your options are limited, you have a good chance of placing in the money. Normally, you should play tighter around the bubble and looser in the money, but when you are short-stacked you only have one option—playing hyperaggressively. You want to prey on the average-stacked blinds, attacking them at every opportunity. You still have enough chips to inflict damage on their stacks and they will be the ones most afraid of being the bubble boy.

When you are short-stacked you only have two options when playing a hand—moving all in or folding. You will have to move all in when you raise since you will be pot-committed anyway. Also, moving all in will give you more fold equity.

There are also times when you should be more selective with your short stack aggression. If you find there is another short stack around the bubble, you should bide your time. Stealing just enough blinds to survive is now your number one priority. You want to force the other short stack into taking the risks. If, however, the other short stack manages to double up, you will find yourself in a bit of trouble and will have to go back to your hyperaggressive style. You might even have to move all in three hands in a row just to survive.

AVERAGE STACK

When you find yourself average-stacked you have to become very selective with your aggression. You don't want to take too many unnecessary risks, but you can't afford to wait around for the short stack to bust out either. In one or two orbits you will find yourself becoming the short stack, so you want to steal blinds just to remain average-stacked. Be selective on whose blinds you steal; you don't have much margin for error. You are only one wrong steal away from becoming short-stacked or eliminated. Try to target another tight medium-stacked player at the table who's just hanging on to get into the money. Normally, the player who is folding his big blind to most raises or the player who hasn't stolen many big blinds from his small blind are the perfect candidates.

Being average-stacked, you will come across many tough decisions at this stage of the tournament. If you find yourself up against one of these decisions and are not sure what to do, folding is usually the correct move. Even if you think you are ahead in the hand, you still have a chance of becoming short-stacked or busting out of the tournament. Ask yourself: "Do I have to get involved in the hand?" Don't be scared to fold, there will be plenty more stealing opportunities.

EXAMPLE

The blinds are $150/$300. A player with $2,000 moves all in from the button. You are in the big blind with $1,900 and have pocket sevens. This would seem like a tough decision but if you look at it closely it's an easy fold. If your opponent is raising with a higher pair, you are in bad shape. Even if your opponent only has a 10-8, it is still 50-50. Folding would be the correct move here. You only lose the big blind and are still in the tournament.

If you find there is an aggressive big stack who is playing every hand, don't think it's your job to put him in his place. Instead, sit back and let him knock someone out or double him up. Either way you have lost nothing and still have a chance of getting into the money.

If you find everyone has the same size stack at this stage of the tournament, the way you should play will depend on the type of table you are up against. Usually, you should play the opposite of what everyone else is doing. If the game has become aggressive with everyone raising, you should tighten up and play premium hands only. If the game become tight, you should loosen up and become more aggressive in your play.

If you find there are two short stacks around the bubble, you should change your strategy again. Tighten up your play since there are now two players who have to survive and you are in a great position to just stroll into the money.

These are just some of the different situations, more of which are mentioned in the next section, that may occur around the bubble. It is your goal to recognize these situations and take advantage of them.

BIG STACK
When playing with a big stack, aggression will reap rewards due to the tight styles your opponents will adopt around the bubble. If the game is tight, which will happen most of the time, you should build your stack by constantly stealing the blinds and bullying the other players at the table with aggressive play. Stealing blinds and building your stack will put you in a great position to go on and win the tournament.

Avoid confrontations with any other big stacks. However, if you find there is a tight big stack, don't be scared to raise since he will be just as scared of going against you as you are of him. The key when raising another big stack is to make it look like you are willing to go all in but not really commit yourself to the pot. Raising a third of your stack will have this effect. If the big stack does decide to play back he will have to move all in. Now you know he has a hand and you can fold. The big stack will have to put his tournament life on the line while you only commit one-third of your stack. Warning: I only recommend this strategy against a tight big stack opponent since you will find that a loose big stack player will play back at you too often to make these raises profitable.

When you are big-stacked, it is your job to bully the small and average stacks. Overbetting the pot preflop is a powerful strategy which forces your opponents to jeopardize their whole stack when getting involved with you. If you decide to call an all in around the bubble, a short stack's all in is to your advantage whereas an average stack's is a disadvantage. This is because the average-stacked players can inflict more damage. Apart from this, almost every situation when you are big-stacked around the bubble is to your advantage.

Below are some situations that can be taken advantage of.

SMALL BLIND NEXT TO AVERAGE STACK

When you are in the small blind and are next to an average-stacked big blind, you should raise every time since the average stack will be scared of a confrontation with you. This will work best when there is a short stack at the table, making the average stack even more reluctant to get involved in a hand with you since he knows the short stack is nearly out.

AVERAGE STACK RAISING WITH A SHORT STACK YET TO ACT

If the average stack raises and there is a short stack acting after you, you can reraise all in with any cards. The average stack will only call with a premium hand because he will know that the short stack will soon be out. However, make sure your reraise has fold equity. If your opponent raises more than half his stack you won't be able to push him off his hand.

TWO SHORT STACKS

Another situation that may occur is when two short stacks are hanging on to get into the money. This is a perfect time to apply pressure to the average stack at the table. He knows the short stacks are just hanging on, forcing the average stack to fold everything apart from premium hands.

SHORT STACKS

When you are the big stack and everyone else is short-stacked, I recommend raising every hand as it now becomes a battle between the short stacks to survive, giving you a license to bully.

However, there is an exception to always bullying the small and medium stacks. When you're the big stack, you don't really want the bubble to end. Once you are in the money your opponents become harder to push around. In certain situations, folding to a short stack's big blind can be more beneficial to you than raising.

EXAMPLE

The blinds are $100/$200, under the gun has $1,200, the button has $1,000 and you are in the small blind with $7,500. The big blind only has $500. Under the gun and the button fold. In this situation you should fold since the big blind is committed to his hand and folding here will mean you can keep bullying the other stacks at the table.

There are some other important bubble concepts you should know and I have outlined them below.

FOLD EQUITY

When you raise or reraise around the bubble stage of a tournament, the main factor you have to take into account is the fold equity you have with your raises.

Fold equity is the chance you have of making your opponent fold. The more chips you raise with, the more fold equity you have. Below is a chart taking into account the fold equity you would have when raising all in against different size stacks.

The table does not take into account the different playing styles of your opponents, which is an important factor affecting your fold equity. If you move all in on a tight average stack you will have a higher fold equity than if you move all in on a loose average stack.

The table is just a device to help you understand fold equity in more depth. It should never be used alone when making your decisions.

FOLD EQUITY

Your Stack	Against a Short Stack	Against a Medium Stack	Against a Big Stack
Short	Medium	Medium	Low
Medium	High	High	Medium
Big	High	High	High

It is worth noting that if you have been caught bluffing you will have low fold equity with future raises, since players won't give you credit for a hand.

TEAMING UP

This is one of the most important concepts you need to know around the bubble. **Teaming up** is when you call an all in with a weak hand after somebody has already called. What you are doing by calling is giving yourself more chances of getting into the money. With two players now in the pot (the first caller and you), there is a better chance of one of you flopping something and busting the all-in player.

EXAMPLE

A player under the gun moves all in with

The button calls with

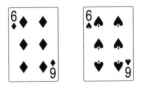

You are in the big blind with

It's only $500 more, so you should call. If you don't, the all-in player will have a 49 percent chance of winning the hand and doubling up, but if you also call, he will only have a 35 percent chance of winning the hand. This gives you a 65 percent chance of getting in the money, 16 percent more than if you would have folded. The rule of thumb is that if it costs only a small amount more to call, you should call.

When you team up on a player, you should try to check the hand to a showdown, even if you do connect with the flop. Checking will give the other caller free cards to catch a hand that might beat the all-in player. You should never bluff when teaming up on someone. The example below demonstrates why.

EXAMPLE

The all-in player has

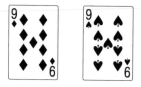

The small blind that called has

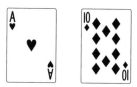

And you call with

The flop comes

You now have top pair. If you bet here you will force the small blind to fold and lose the hand, doubling up the all-in player. However, if you just check it down you are giving the small blind the chance to catch an ace or ten on the turn or river to beat the all-in player's pair of nines.

The only real time you can bet your hand is if you have a strong enough holding that guarantees you will beat the all-in player. Top pair is usually not strong enough. Two pair or a set would be the minimum requirement to make betting okay.

THE GOLDEN RULE

This rule is so important I have called it the golden rule for the bubble. Read it to yourself over and over again:

> **THE GOLDEN RULE**
>
> *Whoever raises the pot has the right to take it down.*

I can't emphasize this enough, especially with a medium or short stack. You need a much stronger hand to call a raise with than you would need to raise with in the first place. Learning the Golden Rule is a big step towards playing perfect preflop poker, which is critical around the bubble.

POT ODDS

To find out the pot odds you are getting when involved in a hand, you have to divide the size of the pot by how much it costs to call.

EXAMPLE 1

The pot contains $600. A player moves all in for $300, so it now costs $300 to call. You are getting 3 to 1 because the pot ($900) divided by the cost to call ($300) equals 3 to 1.

EXAMPLE 2

You have $3,000 in chips, the blinds are $200/$400, you raise to $800. The button has $1,400 and moves all in. Everyone else folds and the action's back on you. To figure out what odds you are getting to call the re-raise, divide the pot by how much it costs to call. The pot would be $200 plus $400 equals $800 plus $1,400. So it would be $2,800 (the pot size) divided by $600 (the amount of the call), which equals pot odds of 4.6 to 1.

Now that you know how to calculate your pot odds, what you need to know is that around the bubble, when you are getting 2 to 1 or higher to call an all-in preflop raise and it's not putting your tournament life on the line, you should call. This means that when you call, you only need a 33 percent chance of winning to make your call mathematically correct. Many hands will have a higher winning percentage than this.

SUMMARY

You should play tighter on the bubble but looser when in the money.

If you find yourself having to make a marginal decision on the bubble, the correct move is to fold. Even if you think you are ahead in the hand, you still risk the chance of going out of the tournament.

Always be aware of your opponents' stack sizes in relation to the blinds.

Always be aware of when the next level of blinds is approaching.

The way you play is determined by the size of your stack and the types of players you are up against.

You should only call raises with premium hands.

When a raise has already been called, you need an even bigger hand to call.

Whoever raises it first has the right to take it down.

Don't expect to make the money every time you reach the bubble. Sometimes you just won't get dealt enough good cards or your big hand won't hold up. That's poker.

9. IN THE MONEY (ITM)

Your game plan when entering a sit-and-go is to reach the last three places, where the money is distributed. Many beginners make the mistake of trying to win the tournament early on in the sit-and-gos, but you shouldn't try to do this until you are in the money. When you do get to the last three players, your game plan can change. You will find there is a considerable difference in the prize pool between first and third, so the best strategy now that you are in the money is to go for first and settle for third.

Here's why. If you come in the money in ten sit-and-gos, each with $10 buy-ins, and come in third place six times, second place three times and first place once, you will have made a profit of $160 ($260 in winnings less $100 entry fee). However, if you win just three of them and come third in the rest, you will have made a profit of $190. That's $30 more, nearly the equivalent of winning another tournament.

HYPERAGGRESSIVE PLAY

To win a lot of tournaments you will have to become hyperaggressive in your play, raising at least 70 percent of your hands when you're in the money. When you do raise, I recommend moving all in to get the most fold equity. Playing this aggressively should win you the blinds a couple of times in a row. You will then be able to risk a 50-50 situation with an opponent to put his tournament life on the line but not yours.

EXAMPLE

You are in a ten man sit-and-go and you all start off with $1,000 in chips. You manage to get your stack up to $2,750 by the time you reach the last three places. The blinds are $250/$500. You are on the button and move all in. Both blinds fold and you pick up $750. Next hand you are in the big blind and both opponents fold. Now you have $4,250, about 50 percent of the chips in play.

Next hand, the button folds and you are in the small blind. You try another steal and move all in. This time the big blind with $2,000 in chips calls. If you lose the confrontation you will still have $2,000 and can start your hyperaggressive style again. But if you win the confrontation you will have a massive chip lead going into heads-up play.

Even if you are short-stacked, don't play scared. You have already made a profit so go for broke. With such high blinds it only takes two successful steals and you are average-stacked again.

The key to this style of play is that when you raise, you are the first one entering the pot. Not being the first in will only compromise the strategy. If someone else is doing the bullying, you will have to make a stand sooner rather than later, since you can't afford to let someone else dominate the game and gain a huge chip lead.

IN THE MONEY SUMMARY

This is the first time your main objective changes to winning the tournament.

You should play looser and more aggressively when in the money.

You should move all in with mediocre hands but not call all ins with mediocre hands.

Don't let another player gain a massive chip lead.

Never give up even if you are short-stacked.

10. HEADS-UP

If you play the way I recommend, you will either go out in third place or have the chip lead going into heads-up play. When you have the chip lead you want to play heads-up aggressively, applying the pressure at every chance you get. You want to put the questions to your opponent, forcing him to make the tough decisions.

An important aspect of heads-up play is that your starting hand requirements become very loose. Any pair, aces, and kings become massive hands. Jack-high is the average dealt hand in heads-up play, which shows you what hands you should now play aggressively.

STRATEGY

When you have a big stack, any two cards are good enough to raise all in with. There will be so many chips to win through the high cost of blinds and antes that you can't go wrong by pushing. Even if you move all in with 7-2 and your opponent calls with A-K, you will win the tournament 33 percent of the time. More importantly, it will put your opponent's tournament life on the line, not yours. If you do manage to steal the blinds two to three times in a row, you will be in a good position to call the remainder of your opponent's chips with any two random cards.

Another advantage to playing this aggressively is that it forces your opponent to make more mistakes in his own play due to the frustration of being pushed around. Throughout this book you will see the reccurring theme of aggression. There are endless benefits from this style of play, the most important being that it is the only way to be a consistent winner in no-limit hold'em, especially during heads-up play.

When you and your opponent are about even in chips, you have to be selective with your aggression. Playing the player comes even more into the equation. If your opponent is tight, you take control of the game by raising and being more aggressive. Just by stealing the blinds a few times, you can become the chip leader and can start playing a big stack strategy.

If you find yourself up against an aggressive player, you will still need to apply pressure, but you should also be more selective with the hands you play. The key to playing an aggressive player is to not let him get the upper hand. If you feel yourself falling behind, don't be afraid to take a stand and move all in at the next opportunity you get. When you find your opponent is raising every hand, you have to ask yourself: "Can I afford to let go of the hand?" Normally, when your opponent begins to have around 70 percent of the chips in play, you will have to make a stand. Not doing so will only lead to you having to call for the remainder of your chips with any two random cards.

When you find yourself short-stacked, you need to find the best opportunity to move all in and hope for a double up. The smaller your stack gets, the more hands you should be willing to go all in with. Remember that even if your opponent has a three to one chip lead over you, you are still only two double ups from being even.

No matter the size of your stack, when you do decide to play a hand, you should either raise or fold. Never limp in since this only represents weakness and gives your opponent the perfect opportunity to make a move on you. The only time it might be acceptable to limp is if you have a premium hand and are trying to trap an aggressive player. I don't recommend seeing flops in heads-up play as the blinds are so high. You can't afford to call a raise preflop and then let go of your hand on the flop.

Often in heads-up play, the winner will be decided by two premium hands meeting each other. That's why if you have been playing aggressively you can afford to get unlucky and still be in the tournament with all the extra chips you have accumulated.

EXAMPLE

You and your opponent are even in chips with $5,000. The blinds are $300/$600. You manage to steal the blinds twice by playing aggressively. Now you have $6,800 and your opponent has $3,200. Next hand, your opponent moves all in with

You call with

No matter how many times you play this hand, both of you are going be to be going all in. But the advantage of playing aggressively means you now can afford to lose the confrontation and still be in the tournament.

SUMMARY

Aggression is key.

When you are big-stacked, playing your stack becomes more important than playing your cards.

Don't let yourself become short-stacked.

The way you play an average stack depends on the type of opponent you are up against.

Limping should never be done unless you are slow-playing a premium hand.

11. AFTERTHOUGHT

After each tournament you should analyze the way you have played. If you busted out of the tournament, think back and see what you could have done differently. Analyze what hand you went out on, how you played it, and if you could have done something different. Ask yourself if you should have raised more preflop, checked the river on a particular hand, or made different types of decisions.

Too many players are willing to blame the luck of the cards or say they got a bad beat without looking at the fact that they played badly. I can't tell you the number of bad beat stories I hear from friends saying they flopped two pair with 9-7 and the other guy had trips—but they always forget to mention they called a raise from there big blind with that 9-7 offsuit. Learning from your mistakes is how you improve your skill; it is also the main factor that separates good poker players from great ones.

12. TYPES OF PLAYERS

When playing a hand, knowing the type of player you are up against can be just as important as the cards you are playing. In sit-and-gos, you will come across many different types of opponents, each one having his own unique way of playing. It's your job to find out what that way is. If you can figure out your opponents' playing styles, you will have a big advantage when playing hands against them.

Following are small descriptions of the types of players you might find at your tournament table.

TIGHT-AGGRESSIVE

Tight-aggressive players fold a lot of hands preflop, but when they are involved in a hand, they play it aggressively. They are not afraid to bluff or make a play. Their decisions are usually based on their hand and the betting patterns of their opponents. The best way to play against tight-aggressive players is to try and pick up on their betting patterns and using these patterns against them. Varying your play is critical against these type of players. Occasionally playing your hand the opposite of how you normally would will throw them off.

Tight-aggressive is the type of player you should be in the early stages of a tournament. You won't come across many players like this in the lower limits, but there will occasionally be a few.

HYPERAGGRESSIVE

Hyperaggressive players like to bet, raise, and re-raise. They play **bottom pair** (a pocket card that forms a pair with the lowest card on board) as aggressively as top pair, making them almost impossible to read. They are either one of the first out of the tournament or have a big stack in the latter stages, becoming very dangerous opponents. These types of players can become a problem, especially if you find one to the left of you, because of the constant reraising you will encounter when you try to steal the blinds. When faced with a hyperaggressive player, you should tighten up your hand selection before getting involved in a pot with him. Capitalize on the overaggressive style of hyperaggressive players by trapping them and slowplaying on the flop.

In the later stages of a tournament you want to change gears and become this type of player preflop. This will help you steal more blinds and build a bigger stack.

CALLING STATIONS

Calling stations never think of what their opponents might have. They don't show much aggression and prefer to just call rather than raise or reraise. It's hard to read these types of players because they will flat call with two pair or bottom pair. They can often be found in the later stages of a tournament with big stacks as a result of being bluff proof and because they've gained chips by constantly calling other players' bluffs.

The best strategy to use against calling stations is to play solid poker and to avoid bluffing or complicated moves. Bet aggressively when you make a hand and try to check it if you don't. Top pair or **middle pair** (a pocket card that forms a pair with a card that is neither the highest nor lowest on the board) are all good enough hands to play aggressively. Avoid stealing calling stations' blinds unless you are willing to go all in.

LOOSE

Loose players bet and raise with mediocre hands in any position. They stay in every hand until the showdown and are willing to chase flush and straight draws no matter how expensive it is. Although they can get lucky, loose players generally lose more money than they win. When you make a hand against a loose player, you should play it aggressively. That will make the most of his loose call. Not much separates the skill levels of loose players from calling stations, apart from the fact that loose players raise more and play more hands.

WEAK-TIGHT

Weak-tight players fold most hands preflop, but when they do play a hand it's usually a premium one. This makes it easy for you get a read on them. If they hit something on the flop, they bet; if they don't, they check. When involved in a hand against weak-tight players, you should usually bet every flop since your opponents won't connect two-thirds of the time. This means you will win more than you lose. There will normally be a couple of weak-tight players left in the later stage of a tournament due to their overly tight style. Weak-tight players will become even tighter when getting close to the money. Ideally, you want this type of player to the left of you so you can capitalize on their conservative style by stealing the blinds.

LOW LIMIT IMAGE

In general, you want to play against solid players who can make intelligent laydowns. Most of the lower limit sit-and-gos are full of weak opponents who are bluff-proof, forcing you to play solid A-B-C poker. Although knowing your own table image is important in poker, in the lower-limit tournaments you will find that the other players at the table are of a poorer standard and won't even have a strategy, let alone know your table image. So don't base many of your poker decisions on what you think they think that you have.

13. BASIC CONCEPTS

In this chapter I will discuss some concepts you need to know when playing sit-and-gos. These topics include some basic strategy rules that you need to learn before you sit down and play.

PREFLOP RAISING

There are many reasons for raising with a hand. One reason is to thin down the field when you have a premium hand, making it expensive for trash hands to see a flop, and giving you more chances of winning. Another reason for raising is to take some of the guesswork out of poker. You gain valuable information on your opponents' hands by the way they react to your raise. When you raise, you want that raise to represent a significant amount of your opponents' stacks. That way it means something to them if they decide to play; the raising will restrict them to only playing good hands (and not connecting with drawing or junk hands after the flop, which can hurt you)—and folding weaker ones.

In the early stages of the tournament when the blinds are small ($10/$20), a raise of three times the big blind is not going to mean much to anyone's stack. Because of this, you have to change your raises for the different stages of the tournament. Below are some guidelines on how much you should raise preflop during the different stages.

Early stages:	4 ½ times the big blind
Middle stages:	3 times the big blind
Later stages:	2 ½ times the big blind

For example, if you raise in the first round of play when the blinds are $10/$20, you'd make it $90 to go.

If there have already been callers before you get to raise, the rule of thumb is to raise the amount of the big blind plus add the value of the limpers' bets.

EXAMPLE

It's in the middle stage of a sit-and-go, the blinds are $25/$50, and there are three limpers. You should raise $300. That is $150 ($50 for each limper) plus three times the big blind for $150 more—a total of a $300 raise.

The main benefit of always raising the same amount at a certain stage of the tournament is that it avoids giving away any information about your hand based on the bet size that is made.

BETTING ON THE FLOP

You will be making all your critical decisions on the flop. With the small amount of chips you are given in sit-and-go tournaments, there is not much turn and river play. If you are aggressive, it will make a lot of these tough decisions easier. Being the aggressor will not only put your opponents on the defensive but also give you valuable information about their hands by the way they react to your betting.

EXAMPLE
The blinds are $100/$200. You are on the button and raise to $600 with

Your opponent in the big blind calls. The flop comes

Your opponent checks. Now you have the option to check or bet. I will run both scenarios to illustrate which one leads to the best outcome.

OPTION 1: CHECKING ON THE FLOP
You check and the turn comes

Now you have caught a pair. Your opponent decides to bet $600. What do you do? You don't really know where you are at in the hand. Your opponent could have been trying to check-raise you on the flop, but he also could easily be reading your check on the flop as weak and trying a stone cold bluff.

You decide to call, the river comes

The 8 shouldn't bother you. If you thought your **second pair** (when one of your pocket cards forms a pair with the second-highest card on board) was good on the turn, then you should still think you're ahead. Your opponent bets out for $800. Again it could be a bluff or your opponent could be value betting his aces. Either way you don't really know. You decide to call as you do have a pair. Your opponent turns over A-5 and you have lost $2,000 through calling.

OPTION 2: BETTING OUT ON THE FLOP

Same situation as before, but instead of checking the flop you decided to bet the flop. After all, you did show strength preflop and your opponent should be just as scared of the ace if he didn't have one. You bet $700 and your opponent reraises you all in. That's not what you wanted but you did get the answer you were looking for. You lose $1,300. That's $700 less than you would have lost if you just check-called to the river.

CONCLUSIONS

Now that you know that being aggressive on the flop leads to the best outcome, you have to decide how much you are going to bet. If you have a hand, you want to raise enough to make it expensive for someone with a draw to call, and you also want it to be enough so that when you do get called it builds the pot considerably. A bet of around 70 percent of the pot will do all this. But more importantly, if you are bluffing it won't commit too many chips to the hand. Again, always betting the same amount will make it impossible for your opponents to put you on a hand. Sometimes you will find your opponent will call you down to the river with as little as second pair not knowing if you are just bluffing again or if you actually have the goods.

If an opponent has already become the aggressor, don't be afraid to reraise if you think you have the best of it. Due to the small amount of chips you are given in sit-and-gos, reraising can be a bit of a problem. It commits a lot of chips to the hand, so it's best done when you are holding a good hand or at the very least, a strong semibluff.

If your bet on the flop is more than half of your stack, you should move all in since you will be pot-committed to the hand anyway. A great advantage of moving all in on the flop is it stops your opponent from having the option of making a play and reraising, pushing you off the hand.

FLOP CONSIDERATIONS

Whenever you see a flop, you should analyze the texture of it. Make your betting decision based on the way your opponent reacts to your betting. Every flop should be treated differently. Here are some guidelines that apply to flop play.

KEY FLOP CONCEPTS

Top pair should be played aggressively because of the structure of sit-and-go tournaments.

Anytime you are prepared to check and call, it is better to bet in the first place.

If you are check-raised, you are usually up against a decent hand.

If a player makes a minimum raise on the flop, it normally means he is trying to steal the pot cheaply.

Always be aware of the other players acting behind you.

TURN CONSIDERATIONS

On the turn, your options are limited due to the structure of sit-and-go tournaments. If you raised preflop and then bet on the flop, you will be pot-committed by the time you get to the turn. However, there are a few rules that still can be applied.

KEY TURN CONCEPTS

If you're heads-up in a hand and your opponent checks the flop and turn, you should bluff 90 percent of the time since your opponent has shown weakness in both betting rounds.

In general, you should stop slowplaying after the turn.

RIVER CONSIDERATIONS

The river is played the same as the turn apart from a few exceptions.

If an opponent bets small into a big pot on the river, you should call since he could be bluffing and you will be receiving favorable odds, making the call correct.

If you are reraised with a medium-strength hand on the river, you are probably behind.

If you have bluffed the flop and turn and been called each time, you should cut your losses and check it down.

Don't bet on the river if the only reason you will be called is because your opponent has a better hand.

EXAMPLE

The board cards are

You have

This gives you a pair of jacks on the river. Instead of betting you should just check it to a showdown. If you did bet, the only time you will get called or reraised is when your opponent is holding a flush, a 3, or a 7. Obviously, this doesn't apply to every hand, but when you do bet the river you should always ask yourself: What am I trying to achieve with my bet?

BETTING PATTERNS

A **betting pattern** describes how a player bets when involved in a pot. Analyzing betting patterns is the best way to read your opponents' hands when playing poker, particularly the online version. Most players that compete in the lower limit sit-and-gos have a fixed way of playing, which can be picked up on. You should try to discover any patterns they might have. For example, pay attention to see if they check-raise top pair or come out betting, if they limp in with big hands or raise with them, etc. All this information will help you get a better read on your opponents.

One of the best tips I can give about betting patterns is something that Mike Caro pointed out many years ago: When someone acts strong it usually means they are weak, and when they act weak it usually means they are strong.

CARDOZA PUBLISHING ◆ NEIL TIMOTHY

EXAMPLE

The blinds are $25/$50. A player in late position moves all in for $3,000. You are in the big blind with

Normally, in the early stages of the tournament when the action is crazy preflop, I would fold jacks. However, an all-in preflop raise in a sit-and-go tells me a number of things about my opponent's hand. First, it tells me that he doesn't have aces, kings, or queens, because someone with one of those hands would want to keep me in the pot, not scare me off. In fact, that all in is telling me the complete opposite. It looks like my opponent doesn't want to see a flop with his hand, which would have me thinking he has a low pocket pair like eights or nines, in which case I would be a huge favorite, so I would call.

EXAMPLE

This time you have $3,000 and the blinds are $100/$200. You are on the button and make it $600 with

106 How to Beat Sit-and-Go Poker Tournaments

The big blind, also with $3,000 in chips, calls with

The flop comes

Your opponent moves all in, giving you what seems like a tough decision. However, if you go through the thinking described above, you will see it is not actually that tough of a decision. If you try to put your opponent on a hand you will see that his betting doesn't add up. If your opponent was holding an ace with a strong kicker, he would properly have reraised preflop. More important though, is that if he had an ace with a weak kicker, he would probably go for a check-raise. Also, his all-in bet is odd. There is $1,500 in the pot and the all-in bet is $2,400. If he had anything, he would want to keep you in the hand, properly betting around $700 (half the pot). The raise is a scared bet which doesn't want a call. I would be more scared of a check here than an all in. In fact, I would put my opponent on a semibluff, not bottom pair.

In the lower limits, you will find that your opponents are not very skillful and, for the most part, they won't be trying to pick up on any patterns you might have. Occasionally, you will come across better opposition who will try to exploit your betting patterns. If this happens, you will need to mix up your play and vary your style. Instead of always betting top pair, you should try a check-raise once in a while or come out betting when you hit a monster. This will stop you from becoming too predictable. Bear in mind this will only occassionally happen and playing solid poker is all that is really needed for you to come out on top in the lower-limit tournaments.

PUTTING OPPONENTS ALL IN

Leaving an opponent with a small amount of chips is a fundamental mistake made by a lot of inexperienced players. Whenever you raise a player and he has only a few remaining chips left, push him all in. Whenever you leave an opponent with chips, you are giving him a chance to come back into the tournament. Also, you are not getting the full value out of your hand. I've seen countless players leave an opponent with $100, thinking it's only a matter of time before that player busts out, only to see the same player double up four times in a row and go on to win the tournament.

14. PLAYING FROM THE BLINDS

Playing from the blinds can be a problem for most beginners. The fact that chips are already invested into the pot sometimes badly influences decisions. In this chapter I will describe the different situations that may occur when playing from the small and big blind positions during a sit-and-go tournament.

EARLY STAGES

In the early stages of the tournament, the blinds will be small. Because of this, you should fold most hands preflop when your blinds are raised. There is no need to get involved in a hand when you only have the minimum invested. Of course, if it's a flat raise (double the big blind), you should usually call since you will be getting the right odds to catch a massive flop with your random hand. This also applies when you are in the small blind and there have been no preflop raises.

Again, you will be getting the right odds to justify a call.

Another benefit of making up the small blinds in the early stages of tournaments is it stops you from being marked as a tight player, keeping your opponents from attacking your blinds in the later stages of the tournament.

MIDDLE AND LATER STAGES

In the later stages of the tournament, when the game becomes short-handed, it can be trickier playing from the blinds. You should still give up your blinds to most raises. However, if you feel an aggressive player is consistently stealing your big blind, you will have to make a stand sooner rather than later.

Earlier, I described what stealing hands were and how they should only be played when no one else has raised, but there is an exception. If an aggressive player has raised your blinds a couple of times in a row from a good position and you find a stealing hand, you can draw a line in the sand and reraise. It's important that you have a stealing hand when reraising since a lot of the time when you are raising you will have to move all in. Your stealing hand is Plan B if you get called.

For reraising from your big blinds to be correct, the following criteria need to be met:

1. You have high fold equity with your reraises.
2. The original raiser raised from a good position (sign of a steal).
3. The raiser is an aggressive player.

The main benefit of reraising from the blinds is that you can acquire a lot of chips without having to see a flop. It also make your opponents cautious about stealing your blinds in the future.

MAKING TOP PAIR FROM YOUR BLIND

If you have played the tight strategy recommended in this book, the only time you will see a flop in the early stages of a tournament is when you play from your blinds. This, however, can lead to problems of its own. Seeing the flop with rubbish cards makes it hard to know where you are in a hand, especially when you connect with the flop.

Top pair should usually be played aggressively in sit-and-gos, but there is an exception. If, in the early stages of a tournament, you make top pair in an unraised multiway pot, you will have to play it with caution. You have no read on anyone else's hands and you could have easily made a second-best hand. If you feel you are behind in the hand don't be afraid to fold. The worst thing that can happen in a sit-and-go tournament is to go out in the early stages.

When you do connect with the flop from your blinds, the way to play it is to put out a feeler bet to see where you are in the hand.

EXAMPLE
You are in the big blind with

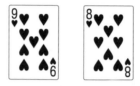

The button and small blind have limped in. You check and the flop comes

The small blind checks. That's not a bad flop for you. With only one overcard, you should bet out and see what information you can get from the other players. The button folds and the small blind makes a minimum reraise. Now you will have to put your opponent on a hand. It's unlikely your opponent is bluffing, since most players who check-raise have strong hands.

Remember, your opponent limped in from the small blind, so he could have a whole range of hands. His play screams to me, minimum, two pair or trips. You fold and your opponent shows 8-4.

Whenever an opponent makes a bet you have to ask yourself what he is trying to achieve with his bet. Normally a bet like this wants to keep you in the hand for cheap.

Though there is no exact way of putting your opponent on a hand, the way he reacts to your betting and the type of player he is should help you come to your best playing decisions.

In the early stages of a tournament, if you are not sure where you are in the hand, you should consider folding and living to fight another day.

LIMPING ON YOUR BLIND

In the later stages of a tournament, when there are no other players in the hand and the small blind limps in on your big blind, you can make a play and raise with any two cards. The majority of the times the small blind is just trying to see a cheap flop with a weak hand and will fold. When making this move it helps to know the player in the small blind. Obviously, for example, you shouldn't be doing this against a calling station. And make sure the small blind still has enough chips to fold.

The major benefit of this play is that your opponent will be less willing to limp in on your big blind in future hands. I wouldn't recommend this move against a big stack, since he will be more willing to call your raises. And try not to make this play too often in the same tournament because the small blind will not give you credit for a hand every time. He may begin to limp on your blind with premium hands, setting up an expensive trap.

LIMPING ON SOMEONE ELSE'S BLIND

When you limp on someone else's big blind from your small blind you can stop him from making the same play as described above by taking your time when limping. When you call quickly it represent weakness, whereas if you take your time it looks like you had to make a decision on whether to raise or to slowplay a big hand, making your opponent more inclined to just check and see the flop. This also applies when someone decides to steal your big blind. Don't fold straight away. Pretend you have a decision to make and then fold. This may slow down your opponent the next time he tries a steal.

PLAYING FROM THE SMALL BLIND

Sometimes, when I find myself next to a passive large-stacked big blind, I will call the small blind and bet half the pot on the flop no matter what comes. Playing the hand this way stops you from getting into any big confrontations preflop or committing a lot of chips to the hand.

EXAMPLE

You have

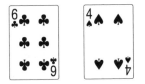

And your opponent has

I can't count the number of times I have pushed all in from the small blind, trying to steal the big blinds, only to be called by an average stack with a hand like this. Avoid the confrontation by just limping in.

You limp in and the flop comes

This is a perfect stealing opportunity since your opponent would have raised preflop with an ace. You now bet half the pot and take the pot uncontested.

PLAYING FROM THE BIG BLIND

The big blind has a lot of leverage when only the small blind has limped in. You have the massive advantage of position on all the betting rounds over your opponent. Whenever it is checked to you on the flop, you can make a stab at most pots since the small blind has shown no strength during the hand. If you decide to check and your opponent checks again on the turn, you should bet every time. Your opponent has shown weakness on two separate betting rounds. Picking up these pots will avoid you from getting blinded away and keep your stack healthy.

SUMMARY

In the early stages of a tournament you should give up your blinds to raises.

Top pair in an unraised multiway pot should be played with caution.

During the later stages of a tournament you should try to play perfect poker from your blinds.

If you are not sure what to do when acting from your blinds, folding is the preferred play.

Most of the time players limp on your big blind to see the flop for cheap.

Keep track of when the next level of blinds is approaching.

15. PLAYS

Plays are specific moves you can use when involved in a hand to outmaneuver your opponents. They can be used to get more chips out of your opponents or to steal pots away from them.

In the early stages of the tournament you will be playing A-B-C poker, but in the later stages you will have to change gears and become more creative in your play. Getting creative will help you steal pots and build your stack. Another reason for making plays in the later stages of a tournament is that there will usually be better players remaining, so your plays will work better against players who can understand your bluffs and make intelligent laydowns.

Below are a number of plays you can use in certain situations against different types of players. Nearly all the plays presented here are most effective against one opponent.

STOP-AND-GO

The stop and go move is one of the best moves at your disposal in sit-and-go tournaments. It is used when someone has raised and you think you are in a 50-50 situation preflop, but feel you cannot push your opponent off his hand by raising all in. It is most effective when you are short-stacked and someone on the button has raised your blind.

If you are holding a pocket pair or a mediocre hand, instead of reraising all in preflop, you call with the intention of pushing all in on the flop no matter what comes. Doing this gives your opponent only three cards, the flop, to catch his hand, whereas if you went all in preflop and got called, your opponent would have five cards—the flop, turn, and river. For the stop-and-go play to work, you need to be the one acting first on the flop so you have the first chance to move all in. The stop-and-go is best done against a tight player who still has enough chips after the flop to be able to fold, and you also need some fold equity with your all-in raise on the flop.

EXAMPLE

It's folded around to the button who raises with

You call from the big blind with

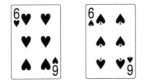

The flop comes

You move all in and your opponent folds, stopping him from catching an ace or king on the turn or river.

PLAYING THE TURN

When you are in a hand heads-up and both you and your opponent have checked on the flop, you can try to pick up the pot by making a bluff if the turn cards comes a blank and you are first to act. A **blank** card is an undercard to the flop that doesn't appear to help any player (for example, gives no one a straight or flush draw). Your opponent may fold even if he has made a pair on the turn since he will be scared of the over-cards already on the board.

I only recommend doing this against a tight player who has shown weakness on the flop. It should never be done against a calling station who will call you down with bottom pair.

EXAMPLE
You limp in from the small blind with

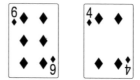

The big blind checks and the flop comes

You check and so does the big blind. The turn comes

This would be an ideal time to make a bluff since the 5 is an undercard, giving no one a flush draw. Even if you do get called you can catch a 3 or 8 to make a straight.

PLAYING WHEN THE FLOP IS PAIRED

When the flop comes paired you can make a play that represents trips. This is a great move for winning small pots but in my experience it can get you in trouble in a big pot. Most players feel unable to let go of their hand when they have a lot of chips invested. The best time to bet a paired flop is when you have shown aggression preflop and get just one caller. The paired flop is an ideal time to bluff your opponent, since there is a good chance he missed it. This play is best done against a tight player who's capable of folding hands.

EXAMPLE

The small blind limps in on your big blind. You have

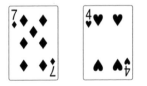

You check and the flop comes

Your opponent bets, indicating that he doesn't have a 6 in his hand since he would have probably slowplayed trips. You have two options. You can either reraise or call with the intention of betting the turn. Your play represents how you would have played with a 6 in your hand. Be careful if the turn comes another 2 as your opponent could have been betting a pair of twos. In my experience, lower-limit players won't let go of their smaller full house.

CHECK-RAISING

Check-raising can be an effective play in the later stages of a tournament as it can commit a lot of your opponent's chips to a hand. It works best against aggressive players who like to make continuation bets on the flop. When going for a check-raise, you have to make sure that giving a free card won't make you a second-best hand just in case your opponent does decide to check.

EXAMPLE

An aggressive player raises on the button and you call from the big blind with

The flop comes

You check and your opponent makes a pot-size bet. You now go over the top of him by reraising. You don't need to have top pair to check-raise an aggressive player. I have done it with as little as bottom pair against a hyperaggressive player who comes out betting on every flop.

It's worth noting that I wouldn't recommend using a check-raise to bluff someone, as it commits a lot of your chips and can be costly if your opponent actually has a hand.

BUTTON STEAL

A **button steal** is a play made when you're on the button and raise with a weak hand when no one else has entered the pot. The object of the raise is to steal the blinds. The steal will have a high success rate because of the small chance of the blinds finding a hand. It's a great move to use to keep building your stack in the later stages of a tournament. It can also be used when you find yourself short-stacked and need breathing space for the next round of blinds.

The major advantage of raising on the button is that if you do get called by one of the blinds, you will still have position over him on the flop.

EXAMPLE

The blinds are $50/$100. The play is folded around and you raise to $300 with

The blinds fold and you collect the pot.

Against tight players, any picture card is good enough to raise with on the button. Be wary if you have raised the last couple of hands, as your raises won't be respected as much.

The disadvantage to a button steal is that it is a common move known by most poker players. You will get played back at frequently, so it helps to know your opponents. It is most effective against tight players who don't defend their blinds. However, loose-aggressive maniacs should be left alone.

SLOWPLAYING

Slowplaying should only be done when giving a free card will not make you a second-best hand.

EXAMPLE

You raise on the button with

The big blind calls and the flop comes

The big blind checks. You have hit a massive hand and there's a good chance your opponent has nothing. If you check, your opponent could catch something on the turn to keep him in the hand.

However, it's different if the flop came

In this situation you shouldn't slowplay. Checking here could let your opponent outdraw you for free. The correct play here would be to bet as there is a flush and straight draw on the board.

SEMIBLUFFING

Semibluffing is betting with a hand you figure may not be the best at the moment, but gives you two ways to win: You can win the pot right there with your bluff, and if you do get called, you can still make your hand. This makes it hard for your opponent to put you on your hand. Semibluffing is best done against a tight opponent who has shown weakness on the flop.

EXAMPLE
You raise preflop with

You get one caller and the flop comes

Your opponent checks to you. If you bet here there's a strong chance your opponent will fold and you will win the pot. But if you are called, you still have plenty of cards that can improve your hand to a winning one. You are actually a favorite against someone with top pair—tens in the above example—in this situation.

DESPERATE ALL IN

If you find yourself short-stacked and one hand away from the next round of blinds (the big blind being to your right), but unable to afford the next round of blinds, you should push with any two cards. The main benefit of moving all in now is that you will still have a bit of fold equity with your all-in raise, whereas you will have no fold equity after the next orbit of blinds have passed through you. This move has more success against an average-stacked blind than a big stack, since it's more costly for the average stack to call.

EXAMPLE

The game has five players left including you. You are to the left of the big blind and have

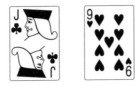

The blinds are $200/$400 and you have $1,000. If you fold and let the blinds go through, you only have $400 left. This means that no matter what hand you decide to play, you only have one way of winning the hand, and that is by winning a showdown. However, if you move all in just before the next round of blinds you will have two ways of winning the hand; either by making everyone fold preflop or by getting called and winning the showdown. This move has a higher success rate on the bubble since there are only three players acting after you and play will tighten around this stage.

STONE COLD BLUFF

A **stone cold bluff** is bluffing with few or no outs. The bluff is best done when you know the type of player you are up against and have some read on him. Stone cold bluffs should be kept to a minimum and should never be used against three or more opponents. They are useful if your opponent has shown weakness up to the river and the only way you can win the hand is by bluffing.

EXAMPLE

You are in the big blind with

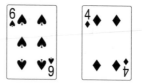

The small blind limps in. You check and the flop comes

Your opponent and you both check. The turn comes

Both of you check again and the river comes

Again your opponent checks. You know if you check, your opponent will probably win the pot with a higher card, so making a bluff here could force him to throw away the winning hand.

LIMPING

Limping with big cards works best in a short-handed aggressive game. If, in the later stages of the tournament, you receive aces, instead of raising you can just call. This is a great way of disguising your hand and giving you the potential to win a large pot. Only make this play when there have been no callers and you feel there is a chance of a raise from an aggressive player.

If it is raised, you have two options. You can either re-raise if you think your opponent will call or just flat call the raise. Calling will make it even harder for your opponent to put you on a big hand, giving you the perfect opportunity to check-raise your opponent for all his chips on the flop. If any other opponents have called the raise, you will have to reraise to stop the pot from becoming multiway. This is the only time you should limp in the later stages of a tournament.

EXAMPLE

You are first to act in an aggressive game and are dealt aces.

The blinds are $150/$300. You have $2,000. You limp in and a player in late position makes it $900 to go, leaving himself with $1,000. Your best move here is to move all in because your opponent's bet indicated he is pot-committed anyway.

EXAMPLE WHEN NOT TO LIMP

The blinds are $150/$300. You are on the button and two players have already limped in from early position. You should now raise with the aces. The pot is big enough already and you don't want to play a multiway pot with your premium hand. Also, somebody might be slowplaying a premium hand as well, which will guarantee you action.

ANOTHER EXAMPLE OF WHEN NOT TO LIMP

You have $700 and the blinds are $150/$300. You are first to act with aces. There's no point in slowplaying in this situation because you only have $400 after you limp. Your best move here is to push all in and hope a big stack calls with a weak hand or the big blind calls with the favorable odds he will be getting. Even if you are not called, just winning the blinds will make a huge difference to your stack.

CONTINUATION BETS

A continuation bet is a standard play that should be used 90 percent of the time when you're heads-up. The idea of a continuation bet is that after you raise with a hand preflop, you bet the flop no matter what comes. Remember, your opponent won't connect with the flop two-thirds of the time, so you will win more pots than you lose.

EXAMPLE

You raise in early position with

A player on the button calls. The flop comes

You bet out and your opponent folds. You win the hand even though you haven't made anything on the flop. Most of the time when you raise you won't connect with the flop, so you should make this bet around 75 percent of the time just to get your chips back.

WHEN NOT TO MAKE CONTINUATION BETS
There are certain times when you shouldn't make continuation bets. If there have been three or more callers preflop, I recommend just checking since there's a good chance that one of your opponents will have connected with the flop. Even if it is checked to you, you should still take a free card since you are running the risk of being check-raised.

DEFENDING AGAINST A CONTINUATION BET
You will find that a lot of players know about continuation bets and make them regularly. To defend against one, you will need to be able to read flops well and know the type of player you are up against. For example, you call a raise and the flop comes

If your opponent bets, there's a good chance he has nothing, since most players will raise with picture cards in their hands. A good way of playing the hand would be to just call the raise on the flop and see what he does on the turn. If he bets again you can be sure he has something. If, however, he checks, you can make a bluff on the river.

It's worth noting that if you are going to defend against a continuation bet with a call, you should have an above-average stack and position so you can gain information on your opponent's hand by how he plays the turn and river.

TAKING THE LEAD

When a player has raised and you have called out of position on the flop, you can come out betting if you think your opponent has hit nothing. You have to remember that your opponent will miss the flop two-thirds of the time, so mathematically, if you bet two-thirds of the pot with your lead you will come out a winner in the long run. Try to make this play against a tight average-stacked player who is capable of folding hands.

DEFENDING AGAINST A WEAK LEAD

This is the same as the play described above apart from your opponent raising into you on the flop after you raised preflop. The way you play the hand will once again depend on the texture of the flop.

For instance, the flop comes

Your opponent bets out. You can be pretty sure your opponent is bluffing, especially if the bet is small, which is a sign of weakness. Most players would check-raise here with overcards or top pair. However, let's say the flop comes

If your opponent bets, there's a good chance he has an ace and is trying to protect against another club coming.

16. ONLINE POKER TELLS

Poker tells are verbal or non-verbal actions which may give away information about a player's hand. Although you can gain information by tells, they can be easily manipulated to disguise a hand, meaning they should never be used solely when making a decision—this goes for online play as well as live games. Online tells are just one of many factors that should be taken into account when deciding what to do in a hand. Below are some online poker tells.

SLOW TO RESPOND

When a player pauses then checks, it usually means he has a medium-strength hand like a flush draw.

When a player pauses a long time and then raises, it could mean he has a strong hand.

QUICK TO RESPOND

A fast check typically means your opponent is using the auto buttons, meaning he has a weak hand.

A quick bet on the turn or river usually means your opponent has a very strong hand.

A quick call when you bet the flop usually means your opponent has some sort of drawing hand.

An automatic minimum reraise preflop usually means your opponent has aces or kings.

BREAK FROM AUTOPLAY MODE

If a player always uses the auto play buttons and a break comes in the pattern, he probably has a big hand.

Remember, online tells can be easily manipulated. Use betting patterns first to figure out what your opponent has, then tells second.

17. TOP 17 TIPS FOR SIT-AND-GOS

1. Patience and discipline are needed for the early stages of the tournament.
2. Only solid tight poker should be played in the beginning.
3. Don't bust out of a tournament in an unraised multiway pot.
4. Premium hands don't play well in multiway pots.
5. Try to leave yourself outs when bluffing.
6. The more opponents you bluff, the less chance you have of being successful.
7. Don't get discouraged if you become short-stacked. I've won countless sit-and-gos with only $50 in chips left.
8. If your raise is more than half your stack, you should move all in.
9. Fold equity is vital when moving all in.

10. Playing the player is just as important as playing your cards.

11. Your hand selection should open up at the later stages of a tournament.

12. You need a better hand to call a raise with, than to raise with in the first place.

13. Position is one of the most important factors in the later stages of a tournament.

14. If during the later stages of a sit-and-go, the table is still full with everyone having around the same amount of chips, it can become a bit of a lottery so choose when to be aggressive and push.

15. Don't expect to get in the money every time.

16. Record keeping is one of the best ways of improving your game.

17. To be successful at sit-and-gos you have to be persistent, always trying to improve your game.

18. COMMON SIT-AND-GO MISTAKES

There are many mistakes made by beginners while playing sit-and-go tournaments. Here are nine of the most common ones. I recommend you learn to identify these mistakes to stop yourself from developing any bad habits.

1. PLAYING TOO MANY HANDS EARLY ON IN A TOURNAMENT

Playing too many hands in the early stages can lead to valuable chips being wasted. If a hand isn't good enough to hold up, fold it. You can afford to do so when the blinds are small.

2. MAKING MINIMUM RAISES WITH PREMIUM HANDS

Whenever you make a minimum raise with a premium hand, you give your opponents the chance to see the flop cheap and bust your big hands. If you have a premium hand, you need to bet appropriately to either scare off some players or to build the pot. This makes it more expensive for opponents to continue playing the round and gives you a greater reward for your big hand.

3. MAKING MINIMUM BETS ON THE FLOP

A minimum bet only shows weakness in your hand. If you are going to make a bet, make sure it is a proper sized one. Whenever you do make a minimum bet on the flop, you allow your opponents to see the turn for cheap, which can lead to you being outdrawn.

4. NOT LETTING GO OF KINGS WHEN AN ACE COMES ON THE FLOP

This is an amateur mistake which can get you into a lot of trouble. When you raise preflop with kings, most players will normally have an ace in their hand when they call, especially if there is more than one caller. Don't be afraid to fold your hand.

5. CALLING AN ALL IN WITH A-K IN THE EARLY STAGES OF A TOURNAMENT

The best thing about A-K is the fold equity you get when playing it. If there is already an all in, you have none. Remember, until the hand improves, all you really have is ace-high.

6. GOING ON TILT

If you can't play your best game when you play poker, how do you expect to have an edge over your opponents? If you receive a bad beat, just brush it off. In the long run, the cards break even and the most skilled player will come out on top.

7. GETTING ATTACHED TO YOUR BLINDS

When you play trash hands from your blinds, you put yourself at a huge disadvantage. Not only do you have to act first on every betting round, but you also put yourself in tricky situations.

EXAMPLE

A player raises from the cutoff. You have

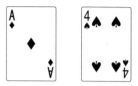

You have to ask yourself what calling will achieve. Remember, you are only going to connect with the flop one-third of the time, meaning most of the time you will be checking to the raiser, giving him the opportunity to bluff you. If your opponent has an ace with a better kicker, you are in bad shape if an ace comes on the flop. If he has a weaker kicker than you, there are now only two aces left in the deck, giving you even less chance of connecting on the flop. Even if you catch a 4, you will be facing overcards on most flops. All these problems can be avoided if you just let go of your blinds and fold.

8. BLUFFING TOO MUCH

Bluffing is a great feeling when it works, but in the lower-limit tournaments, solid poker is the main criteria for success. Don't get me wrong, you do have to make the occasional bluff—just don't overdo it. Bluffing too frequently can get you into trouble.

9. PLAYING WHEN YOU ARE DRUNK

Why would you put yourself at a disadvantage before you even sit down? Every time you decide to play a tournament, you should be able to control your actions. Drinking can only lead to bad judgment and poor decision-making. It gives every one of your opponents an advantage over you, and that's the last thing you want.

19. MULTITABLING

Multitabling is playing more than one sit-and-go tournament at the same time. I would only recommend doing this when you have become an above-average player and are confident in your game. When you do decide to multitable, I recommend starting each tournament at different times. When you are about one-third of the way through one tournament, start another one. Then when that sit-and-go is a third of the way through, you can start another, and so on. This stops the action from becoming too hectic during the later stages of the tournaments.

Some sites allow you to play up to 30 tables at the same time but I would recommend sticking to no more than four tables to start with. You can build your way up from there.

Multitabling is a must for any serious poker player wanting to make a living from sit-and-gos, since you need to be making as much money per hour as you can. You will also need a screen which lets you set your resolution to 1,600 x 1,200 or more to allow all the tables to fit on the screen.

There are many advantages and disadvantages to multitabling.

ADVANTAGES

If you are a winning player, playing more tables means making more money faster.

Due to the tight style you adopt in the early stages of a tournament, it can be boring. Multitabling stops this since you will be busy switching between tables.

If you only play one table at a time and don't finish in the money four times in a row, you have wasted around four hours of poker. But if you were multitabling, you would have only lost, at most, an hour of play, since you would have played all four tournaments at the same time.

DISADVANTAGES

Playing more than one tournament can be confusing, resulting in more errors and mistakes.

It's a lot harder to find out what types of players you are up against if you are constantly switching between tables.

Multitabling makes it harder for you to keep track of when the blinds are going up on the different tables.

If you are disconnected while multitabling, your bankroll can be severely damaged.

Some sites don't let you multitable at all.

Multitabling can make sit-and-go tournaments feel repetitive.

20. BANKROLL

You could be the best player in the world, but if you don't have a large enough bankroll you run the risk of ruin. Your bankroll needs to be set to the amount of money you'll need to survive losing streaks. One of the main advantages of sit-and-gos is you only need a small bankroll, compared to cash games where big bankrolls are needed.

You can lose three sit-and-gos in a row, then win one and you are back where you started. Below is my suggesred bankroll requirements for different limits.

Cost to enter Sit-and-Go	Bankroll Needed
$5 + $1	$100 - $140
$10 + $1	$200 - $260
$20 + $2	$400 - $520
$30 + $3	$600 - $780
$50 + $5	$1,000 - $1,300
$100 + $9	$2,000 - $2,400

I recommend avoiding the $5 + $1 tournaments because the **rake**—the commission the poker rooms take from each game—is too high compared to the other tournaments. For sit-and-go tournaments, the rake is normally 10 percent of the entry fee. There are some sites on the Internet that offer rake-back deals, giving you a percentage of your rake back. Just remember, it doesn't matter how big your bankroll is if you are losing money, so read this book again and again until you become a winner.

21. RECORD KEEPING

Record keeping is a good way of finding out how much time you spend playing poker and how much you are winning or losing. It can help you become more focused and improve your game immensely. When keeping records of your play, you have to put all the information in accurately. There is no point in keeping records if you're just going to bend the information to impress your friends, other players or even yourself. Fudging your notes will never improve your game and defeats the whole purpose.

You need to play about 300 tournaments to have an accurate sample of your play. Once you have logged this many sit-and-gos, you can analyze the strengths and weaknesses in your game. Your sample should show you coming into the money around 35 percent of the time. Anything above this is pretty unsustainable and anything below this can be improved on. When you are in the money, you want to come in third around 45 percent of the time, second 20 percent of the time and first around 35 percent of the time. If you are not reaching these figures, try looking at these four common problems.

1. BUSTING OUT ON THE BUBBLE TOO MUCH

If you find yourself busting out on the bubble too much, maybe you are being too aggressive too soon. Try to tighten up until you get into the money. When in the money, you can then become more aggressive in your play, but only then. The bubble is the most important part of the tournament and busting out on it too often can severely damage your profits.

2. GOING OUT IN THIRD POSITION TOO MUCH

If you find yourself going out in third too often you may be playing too tight while in the money. You should aim to come in first place and settle for third. Become hyperaggressive in your play. This means you should aggressively steal the blinds, which in turn will help you build a chip lead over your opponents.

3. NOT HAVING ENOUGH CHIPS LEFT TO MAKE IT INTO THE MONEY

This normally occurs because you are playing too loose in the early stages of a tournament. I recommend you read the "Early Stage Hand Selection" chapter again to tighten up your preflop play. Another reason you may find yourself not having enough chips is because you are playing too tight in the later stages of the tournament, resulting in you being blinded out. If you feel this is the problem, change gears and become more aggressive. I recommend reading the late stages strategy again.

4. COMING IN SECOND TOO OFTEN

The reason for coming in second too often may be that your heads-up play needs improving, but a lot of the time, the winner of sit-and-go tournament is decided on a premium hand meeting a premium hand. Many times it will be 50-50 for first or second. To improve your heads-up play, try to be more aggressive, putting the pressure on your opponent at every opportunity. Another important factor which should affect the way you play heads-up is the type of opponent you are up against. I recommend you reread the chapter on player types.

These points may come across as common sense, but many players go on playing their same game. Not knowing where you are going wrong stops you from capitalizing on the extra profits you could be making.

22. RECOMMENDED READING

No-limit hold'em takes a minute to learn, but a lifetime to master. You should never think you know everything about the game. There are many different sources of information out there to help you improve your play. Here are a number of books that I recommend you read to help you become a better player.

When reading these books, I recommend you study them thoroughly and then select certain areas you may want to focus on. Reread those sections and then try to incorporate them into your play. After applying what you have learned, read them again if you feel you can still improve on those concepts. But don't just read the books—*learn* them.

SUPER/SYSTEM 2 BY DOYLE BRUNSON
Many people have called this book the poker bible. It covers many forms of poker and has a great section

on no-limit hold'em. Although it is directed at cash games, it gives you a great understanding for the game and the attitude you need to play no-limit. It is a must for any serious poker player.

TOURNAMENT POKER FOR ADVANCED PLAYERS BY DAVID SKLANSKY

Although written for multitable tournaments, it's still worth reading for the strategies, concepts, and theories needed when entering tournaments.

HOLD'EM POKER FOR ADVANCED PLAYERS BY SKLANSKY AND MALMUTH

This is one of the best books on the market for hold'em. It goes into great detail on the theories needed to play short-handed successfully, which is vital for the later stages of sit-and-gos. It also teaches the different levels of thinking needed for poker, with a great chapter on how to put your opponents on a hand.

IMPROVE YOUR POKER AND POT LIMIT AND NO-LIMIT POKER BY BOB CIAFFONE

This book contains an excellent article on satellite strategy which can be applied to your sit-and-go game. Although it is not directed at sit-and-go tournaments, it still should be on the bookshelf of any serious poker student.

23. OUTS

Outs are cards that can improve your hand to a winning one. To roughly calculate the percentage of your hand improving to a winning one by the river, multiply your outs by four. To calculate your winning chances after the turn, multiply your outs by two.

EXAMPLE

The flop comes 3-8-2. You have a pair of tens and your opponent has a pair of jacks. You have two outs (the two other tens) so you have about an 8 percent chance of winning the hand (2 x 4).

The actual percentage for that example is 8.4 percent. Below is a chart showing the percentage of making your hand when you have a certain amount of outs after the flop.

Number of Outs	Percentage
20	67.5%
19	65.0%
18	62.4%
17	59.8%
16	57.0%
15 (straight flush draw)	54.1%
14	51.2%
13	48.1%
12	45.0%
11	41.7%
10	38.4%
9 (flush draw)	35.0%
8 (open-ended straight draw)	31.5%
7	27.8%
6	24.1%
5	20.3%
4 (two pair or gutshot draw)	16.5%
3	12.5%
2	8.4%
1	4.4%

24. POKER ODDS

STARTING HAND PROBABILITIES

Hand	Probability of Being Dealt
A-A	220 to 1
K-K, Q-Q, or J-J	72 to 1
10-10, 9-9, 8-8, 7-7, or 6-6	43 to 1
5-5, 4-4, 3-3, or 2-2	54 to 1
A-K suited	331 to 1
A-K offsuit	110 to 1
A-Q or A-J suited	165 to 1
A-Q to A-J offsuit	54 to 1
K-Q suited	331 to 1
K-Q offsuit	110 to 1
Ace with less than jack, suited	35 to 1
Ace with less than jack, offsuit	11 to 1
Any pair	16 to 1
Any two cards suited	3 to 1
Any hand with a pair or an ace	4 to 1

BASIC DATA

Scenario	Probability
Holding a pair before the flop	16 to 1
Holding suited cards before the flop	3.25 to 1
Holding K-K or A-A before the flop	110 to 1
Holding A-K before the flop	81.9 to 1
Holding at least 1 ace before the flop	5.70 to 1
You have four parts of a flush after the flop and you make it	1.86 to 1
You have four parts of an open-end straight flush after the flop and you make a straight flush	10.9 to 1
You have four parts of an open-end straight flush after the flop and you make at least a straight	0.85 to 1
You have two pair after the flop and you make a full house or better	4.97 to 1
You have three of a kind after the flop and you make a full house or better	1.99 to 1
You have a pair after the flop and at least one more of that kind turns up (on the last two cards)	10.9 to 1
You hold a pair and at least one more of that kind flops	7 to 1
You hold no pair, but pair at least one of your cards on the flop	2 to 1
You hold two suited cards and two or more of that suit flop	7 to 1

LONG SHOTS

Scenario	Probability
If you hold suited cards, a flush will flop	118 to 1
If you hold a pair, four of a kind will flop	407 to 1
If you hold 6-5 offsuit, a straight will flop	75 to 1
If you hold 7-5 offsuit, a straight will flop	101 to 1
If you hold 8-5 offsuit, a straight will flop	152 to 1
If you hold 9-5 offsuit, a straight will flop	305 to 1
If you hold 9-8 suited, a straight flush will flop	4899 to 1
If you hold 9-7 suited, a straight flush will flop	6532 to 1
If you hold 9-6 suited, a straight flush will flop	9,799 to 1
If you hold 9-5 suited, a straight flush will flop	19,599 to 1
No one hold an ace or king in a 10-handed game	70 to 1
Heads-up hold'em, both players hold paired aces	270,724 to 1

ABSENCE OF ACES BEFORE THE FLOP, BY NUMBER OF PLAYERS

Number of Players	The Probability That No Player Has an Ace, Including Yourself (%)	If You Have One Ace, the Probability that No Other Player Has an Ace (%)	If You Have No Ace, the Probability that No Other Player Has an Ace (%)
2	71%	88%	84%
3	60%	77%	70%
4	50%	67%	58%
5	41%	58%	48%
6	33%	50%	39%
7	27%	43%	32%
8	21%	36%	25%
9	17%	30%	20%
10	13%	25%	15%

NOTE: You will not hold an ace 85 percent of the time.

25. LAST WORD

Obviously you want to better yourself as a player, which is why you bought this book. Becoming a winning player is a difficult task and takes practice and discipline. You need to arm yourself with the right strategies and frame of mind to approach sit-and-gos with confidence. I wrote this book not just to save you a lot of money, but to give you the knowledge needed to become a consistent sit-and-go winner.

Writing this book helped me improve my own game and I hope it helps you too. With a little bit of luck and hard work you will soon find yourself on the winning side of poker. You can never know enough about no-limit hold'em and sit-and-gos and should always strive to improve your game. There are endless sources of information available to you for improving your no-limit hold'em knowledge. If you are willing to put in the work and dedicate yourself to a winning plan, there is no reason why you can't beat this game.

Good luck and I hope to see you at the tables soon!

GLOSSARY

A-B-C poker: Straightforward by-the-book poker.

All in: Having all one's chips in the pot.

Average stack: Having about the average number of chips.

Bad beat: Having a hand that is a big favorite being defeated by a lucky drawing.

Bankroll: A certain amount of money you have to gamble with.

Bet: To put chips into the pot.

Betting pattern: The way a player bets when involved in a pot.

Big slick: Ace-king as pocket cards.

Big stack: Having about one and a half times the average stack size.

Blank card: An undercard to the flop that doesn't appear to help any player; for example, gives no one a straight or flush draw.

Blind: A forced bet made before the cards are dealt.

Blinded out: To lose most or all of your chips to erosion from the blinds without playing hands.

Bluff: A bet or raise with a weak hand with the intention of making stronger hands fold.

Board: The five open cards shared by all players.

Bottom pair: A pocket card that forms a pair with the lowest card on board.

Bubble: When a tournament reaches the stage where it is one place away from the money. In a sit-and-go, the last three players get paid, so the bubble occurs when are four players are left.

Button steal: To raise from the button with a weak hand when no one else has entered the pot in the hopes of winning the blinds by default.

Button: A round disc that represents the dealer position. The player that occupies that seat.

Buy-in: The amount of money required to enter a tournament.

Call: To put into the pot an amount equal to a previous bet or raise to stay active in a pot.

Caller: A player who calls a bet or a raise.

Check: To not bet but stay active in a hand.

Check-raise: To check and then raise if another player bets.

Chip: Token representing money.

Continuation bet: To bet the flop after raising preflop.

Cutoff Seat: The seat to the right of the button.

Dog: Longshot

Draw out: To improve and win your hand on the turn or river.

Drawing

dead: Drawing to make a hand that cannot win; for example, drawing to a straight when someone has a flush.

Edge: An advantage.

Flop: The first three cards dealt face up and shared by all players.

Flush: Five cards of the same suit.

Fold: To drop out of a pot.

Fold equity: The chance you have of making an opponent fold. The more chips you raise with, the more fold equity you have.

Four of a kind: Four cards of the same rank.

Four-flush: Four cards to a flush.

Four-straight: Four cards to a straight.

Fourth street (turn): The fourth open card on the table.

Free card: A card that a player gets without having to pay anything for it.

Full house: A poker hand containing one pair and three of a kind.

Heads-up: Playing against a single opponent.

Hyper-aggressive player: A player who consistently and aggressively bets, raises and reraises.

Kicker: A side card.

Limp: Call a bet rather than raise.

Loose: Playing a lot of hands.

Maniac: A player who bets and raises recklessly.

Middle pair: A pocket card that forms a pair with a card that is netiher the highest nor lowest on the board.

Multi-tabling: Playing more than one poker game at the same time.

Nuts: The best hand possible at the moment.

On tilt: A player not playing his best game because he is upset.

Outkicked: A hand where the highest pocket card is equal to an opponent's, but the secondary card is lesser in rank.

Outs: Cards that can improve your hand.

Overbet: To bet more than is standard or needed in a particular situation.

Overcard: A card on board that is higher than the pocket pair being held.

Overpair: A pocket pair higher than any card on the board.

Pair: Two cards of the same rank.

Pass: To fold.

Picture cards: Jacks, queens and kings.

Played back: When an opponent raises after you bet or raise.

Pocket card: One of the player's two private hole cards.

Pocket pair: Two cards of equal rank, a pair, held as concealed cards in a player's hand.

Position: Where a player sits relative to the button.

Pot-committed: To have more than half your chips invested in the pot so that you're committed to putting the rest in if raised.

Pot: The total amount of money bet in a hand which is available to be won.

Rag ace: An ace with a weak side card.

Raiser: A player who raises.

Raise: To bet more in a round after another player has already bet.

Rake: An amount retained by the house for its services.

Reraise: To raise after a player has already raised in the round.

River: The fifth and last open card on board.

Second pair: A pocket card that forms a pair with the second-highest card on board.

Semi-bluffing: To bet or raise with a hand you figure may not be the best at the moment, but it gives you two ways to win: You can win the pot with your bluff or if you get called, you can win by improving your hand.

Set: Three of a kind.

Short stack: Having about half the average stack size or less.

Shut down: To discontinue betting or raising to avoid committing more chips to a hand.

Slowplay: To play a massive hand weakly to encourage a bluff or to let an opponent make a hand that will be second-best.

Stealing hands: Hands that you would not normally play aggressively but because of particular circumstances—in a sit-and-go, when the game becomes short-handed—should be played aggressively pre-flop to try to force out opponents and steal the blinds.

Stone cold bluff: To bluff when having few or no outs.

Straight: Five cards in sequence.

Suited connectors: Cards in sequential order and of the same suit.

Suited: Two or more cards of the same suit.

Tell: A characteristic that gives away a players hand.

Three of a kind: Three cards of the same rank.

Tight player: A player who plays only preiumm cards and thus few hands.

Tight: Playing few hands.

Tight-aggressive player: A player that plays few hands but plays them aggressively.

Top pair: A pocket card that forms a pair with the highest card on board.

Trips: Three of a kind.

Turn: The fourth open card on board.

Under the gun: The first player to act in a hand, particularly in the first round of betting.

FREE!
Poker & Gaming Magazines

www.cardozabooks.com

3 GREAT REASONS TO VISIT NOW!

1. FREE GAMING MAGAZINES
Go online now and read all about the exciting world of poker, gambling, and online gaming. Our magazines are packed with tips, expert strategies, tournament schedules and results, gossip, news, contests, polls, exclusive discounts on hotels, travel, and more to our readers, prepublication book discounts, free-money bonuses for online sites, and words of wisdom from the world's top experts and authorities. Also, you can sign up for Avery Cardoza's free email newsletters.

2. MORE THAN 200 BOOKS TO MAKE YOU A WINNER
We are the world's largest publisher of gaming and gambling books and represent a who's who of the greatest players and writers on poker, gambling, chess, backgammon, and other games. With more than 10 million books sold, we know what our customers want. Trust us.

3. THIS ONE IS A SURPRISE
Visit us now to get the goods!

So what are you waiting for?
www.cardozabooks.com

GAMBLER'S BOOK CLUB
Shop online at the Gambler's Book Club in Las Vegas. Since 1964, the GBC has been the reigning authority on gambling publications and one of the most famous gaming institutions. We have the world's largest selection of gambling books— thousands in stock. Go online now!
702-382-7555
www.gamblersbookclub.com

GREAT CARDOZA POKER BOOKS
ADD THESE TO YOUR LIBRARY - ORDER NOW!

DANIEL NEGREANU'S POWER HOLD'EM STRATEGY *by Daniel Negreanu*. This power-packed book on beating no-limit hold'em is one of the three most influential poker books ever written. Negreanu headlines a collection of young great players—Todd Brunson, David Williams. Erick Lindgren, Evelyn Ng and Paul Wasicka—who share their insider professional moves and winning secrets. You'll learn about short-handed and heads-up play, high-limit cash games, a powerful beginner's strategy to neutralize professional players, and how to mix up your play and bluff and win big pots. The centerpiece, however, is Negreanu's powerful and revolutionary small ball strategy. You'll learn how to play hold'em with cards you never would have played before—and with fantastic results. The preflop, flop, turn and river will never look the same again. A must-have! 520 pages, $34.95.

POKER WIZARDS *by Warwick Dunnett*. In the tradition of Super System, an exclusive collection of champions and superstars have been brought together to share their strategies, insights, and tactics for winning big money at poker, specifically no-limit hold'em tournaments. This is priceless advice from players who individually have each made millions of dollars in tournaments, and collectively, have won more than 20 WSOP bracelets, two WSOP main events, 100 major tournaments and $50 million in tournament winnings! Featuring Daniel Negreanu, Dan Harrington, Marcel Luske, Kathy Liebert, Mike Sexton, Mel Judah, Marc Salem, T.J. Cloutier and Chris "Jesus" Ferguson. This must-read book is a goldmine for serious players, aspiring pros, and future champions! 352 pgs, $19.95.

HOW TO BEAT LOW-LIMIT POKER *by Shane Smith and Tom McEvoy*. If you're a low-limit player frustrated by poor results or books written by high-stakes players for big buy-in games, this is exactly the book you need! You'll learn how to win big money at the little games—$1/$2, $2/$4, $4/$8, $5/$10—typically found in casinos, cardrooms and played in home poker games. After one reading, you'll lose less, win more and play with increased confidence. You'll learn the top 10 tips and winning strategies specifically designed for limit hold'em, no-limit hold'em, Omaha high-low and low-limit poker tournaments. Great practical advice for new players. 184 pages, $9.95.

OMAHA HIGH-LOW: How to Win at the Lower Limits *by Shane Smith*. Practical advice specifically targeted for the popular low-limit games you play every day in casinos and online will have you making money, and show you how to avoid losing situations and cards that can cost you a bundle—the dreaded second-nut draws, trap hands, and two-way second-best action. Smith's proven strategies are spiced with plenty of wit and wisdom. You'll learn the basics of play against the typical opponents you'll face in low-limit games—the no-fold'em players and the rocks—and get winning tactics, illustrated hands, and tournament tips guaranteed to improve your game. 144 pages, $12.95.

TOURNAMENT TIPS FROM THE POKER PROS *by Shane Smith*. Essential advice from poker theorists, authors, and tournament winners on the best strategies for winning the big prizes at low-limit rebuy tournaments. Learn proven strategies for each of the four stages of play—opening, middle, late and final—how to avoid 26 potential traps, advice on rebuys, aggressive play, clock-watching, inside moves, top 20 tips for winning tournaments, more. Advice from Brunson, McEvoy, Cloutier, Caro, Malmuth, others. 160 pages, $14.95.

NO-LIMIT TEXAS HOLD'EM: The New Player's Guide to Winning Poker's Biggest Game *by Brad Daugherty & Tom McEvoy*. For experienced limit players who want to play no-limit or rookies who has never played before, two world champions show readers how to evaluate the strength of a hand, determine the amount to bet, understand opponents' play, plus how to bluff and when to do it. Seventy-four game scenarios, unique betting charts for tournament play, and sections on essential principles and strategies show you how to get to the winner's circle. Special section on beating online tournaments. 288 pages, $19.95.

GREAT CARDOZA POKER BOOKS
ADD THESE TO YOUR LIBRARY - ORDER NOW!

THE POKER TOURNAMENT FORMULA *by Arnold Snyder.* Start making money now in fast no-limit hold'em tournaments with these radical and never-before-published concepts and secrets for beating tournaments. You'll learn why cards don't matter as much as the dynamics of a tournament—your position, the size of your chip stack, who your opponents are, and above all, the structure. Poker tournaments offer one of the richest opportunities to come along in decades. Every so often, a book comes along that changes the way players attack a game and provides them with a big advantage over opponents. Gambling legend Arnold Snyder has written such a book. 368 pages, $19.95.

POKER TOURNAMENT FORMULA 2: Advanced Strategies for Big Money Tournaments *by Arnold Snyder.* Probably the greatest tournament poker book ever written, and the most controversial in the last decade, Snyder's revolutionary work debunks commonly (and falsely) held beliefs. Snyder reveals the power of chip utility—the real secret behind winning tournaments—and covers utility ranks, tournament structures, small- and long-ball strategies, patience factors, the impact of structures, crushing the Harringbots and other player types, tournament phases, and much more. Includes big sections on Tools, Strategies, and Tournament Phases. A must buy! 496 pages, $24.95.

HOW TO WIN AT OMAHA HIGH-LOW POKER *by Mike Cappelletti.* Clearly written strategies and powerful advice shows the essential winning strategies for beating Omaha high-low poker! This money-making guide includes more than sixty hard-hitting sections on Omaha. Players learn the rules of play, best starting hands, strategies for the flop, turn, and river, how to read the board for both high and low, dangerous draws, and how to beat low-limit tournaments. Includes odds charts, glossary and low-limit tips. 304 pgs, $19.95.

WINNER'S GUIDE TO TEXAS HOLD'EM POKER *by Ken Warren.* New edition shows how to play every hand from every position with every type of flop. Learn the 14 categories of starting hands, the 10 most common hold'em tells, how to evaluate a game for profit, the value of deception, the art of bluffing, eight secrets to winning, starting hand categories, position, and more! Includes detailed analysis of the top 40 hands and the most complete chapter on hold'em odds in print. Over 500,000 copies sold! 224 pages, $14.95.

KEN WARREN TEACHES TEXAS HOLD'EM *by Ken Warren.* This is a step-by-step comprehensive manual for making money at hold'em poker. 42 powerful chapters teach you one lesson at a time. Great practical advice and concepts with examples from actual games and how to apply them to your own play. Lessons include: Starting Cards, Playing Position, Raising, Check-raising, Tells, Game/Seat Selection, Dominated Hands, Odds, and much more. This book is already a huge fan favorite and best-seller! 416 pages, $24.95.

WINNER'S GUIDE TO OMAHA POKER *by Ken Warren.* Concise and easy-to-understand, Warren shows beginning and intermediate Omaha players how to win from the first time they play. You'll learn the rules, betting and blind structure, why you should play Omaha, the advantages of Omaha over Texas hold'em, glossary, reading the board, basic strategies, Omaha high, Omaha hi-low split 8/better, how to play draws and made hands, evaluation of starting hands, counting outs, computing pot odds, the unique characteristics of split-pot games, the best and worst Omaha hands, how to play before the flop, how to play on the flop, how to play on the turn and river, and much more. 224 pages, $19.95

HOW TO WIN NO-LIMIT HOLD'EM TOURNAMENTS *by McEvoy & Don Vines.* Learn the basic concepts of tournament strategy and how to win big by playing small buy-in events, graduate to medium and big buy-in tournaments, adjust for short fields, huge fields, slow and fast-action events. Plus, how to win online tournaments. You'll also learn how to manage a tournament bankroll and get tips on table demeanor for televised tournaments. See actual hands played by finalists at WSOP and WPT championship tables with card pictures, analysis and useful lessons from the play. 376 pages, $29.95.

GREAT CARDOZA POKER BOOKS
ADD THESE TO YOUR LIBRARY - ORDER NOW!

HOLD'EM WISDOM FOR ALL PLAYERS *By Daniel Negreanu.* Superstar poker player Daniel Negreanu provides 50 easy-to-read and right-to-the-point hold'em strategy nuggets that will immediately make you a better player at cash games and tournaments. His wit and wisdom makes for great reading; even better, it makes for killer winning advice. Conversational, straightforward, and educational, this book covers topics as diverse as the top 10 rookie mistakes to bullying bullies and exploiting your table image. 176 pages, $14.95.

HOW TO BEAT SIT-AND-GO POKER TOURNAMENTS *by Neil Timothy.* There is a lot of dead money up for grabs in the lower limit sit-and-gos and Neil Timothy shows you how to go and get it. The author, a professional player, shows you how to reach the last six places of lower limit sit-and-go tournaments four out of five times and then how to get in the money 25-35 percent of the time using his powerful, proven strategies. This book can turn a losing sit-and-go player into a winner, and a winner into a bigger winner. Also effective for the early and middle stages of one-table satellites.184 pages, $14.95.

CRASH COURSE IN BEATING TEXAS HOLD'EM *by Avery Cardoza.* Perfect for beginning and somewhat experienced players who want to jump right in on the action and play cash games, local tournaments, online poker, and the big televised tournaments where millions of dollars can be made. Both limit and no-limit hold'em games are covered along with the essential strategies needed to play profitably on the preflop, flop, turn, and river. The good news is that you don't need to memorize hands or be burdened by math to be a winner—just play by the no-nonsense basic principles outlined here. 208 pages, $14.95

INTERNET HOLD'EM POKER *by Avery Cardoza.* Learn how to get started in the exciting world of online poker. The book concentrates on Internet no-limit hold'em, but also covers limit and pot-limit hold'em, five- and seven-card stud, and Omaha. You'll learn everything from how to play and bet safely online to playing multiple tables, using early action buttons, and finding easy opponents. Cardoza gives you the largest collection of online-specific strategies in print—more than 6,500 words dedicated to 25 unique strategies! You'll also learn how to get sign-up bonuses worth hundreds of dollars! 176 pages, $9.95

WINNER'S GUIDE TO TEXAS HOLD' EM POKER *by Ken Warren.* New edition shows how to play every hand from every position with every type of flop. Learn the 14 categories of starting hands, the 10 most common hold'em tells, how to evaluate a game for profit, the value of deception, the art of bluffing, eight secrets to winning, starting hand categories, position, and more! Includes detailed analysis of the top 40 hands and the most complete chapter on hold'em odds in print. Over 500,000 copies sold! 224 pages, $14.95.

KEN WARREN TEACHES TEXAS HOLD'EM *by Ken Warren.* This is a step-by-step comprehensive manual for making money at hold'em poker. 42 powerful chapters teach you one lesson at a time. Great practical advice and concepts with examples from actual games and how to apply them to your own play. Lessons include: Starting Cards, Playing Position, Raising, Check-raising, Tells, Game/Seat Selection, Dominated Hands, Odds, and much more. This book is already a huge fan favorite and best-seller! 416 pages, $24.95.

OMAHA HIGH-LOW: Play to Win with the Odds *by Bill Boston.* Selecting the right hands to play is the most important decision to make in Omaha. This is the *only* book that shows you the chances that every one of the 5,278 Omaha high-low hands has of winning the high end of the pot, the low end of it, and how often it is expected to scoop all the chips. You get all the vital tools needed to make critical preflop decisions based on the results of more than 500 million computerized hand simulations. You'll learn the 100 most profitable starting cards, trap hands to avoid, 49 worst hands, 30 ace-less hands you can play for profit, and the three bandit cards you must know to avoid losing hands. 248 pages, $19.95.

DOYLE BRUNSON'S EXCITING BOOKS
ADD THESE TO YOUR COLLECTION - ORDER NOW!

SUPER SYSTEM *by Doyle Brunson*. This classic book is considered by the pros to be the best book ever written on poker! Jam-packed with advanced strategies, theories, tactics and money-making techniques, no serious poker player can afford to be without this hard-hitting information. Includes fifty pages of the most precise poker statistics ever published. Features chapters written by poker's biggest superstars, such as Dave Sklansky, Mike Caro, Chip Reese, Joey Hawthorne, Bobby Baldwin, and Doyle. Essential strategies, advanced play, and no-nonsense winning advice on making money at 7-card stud (razz, high-low split, cards speak, and declare), draw poker, lowball, and hold'em (limit and no-limit).This is a must-read for any serious poker player. 628 pages, $29.95.

SUPER SYSTEM 2 *by Doyle Brunson*. SS2 expands upon the original with more games and professional secrets from the best in the world. New revision includes Phil Hellmuth Jr. along with superstar contributors Daniel Negreanu, winner of multiple WSOP gold bracelets and 2004 Poker Player of the Year; Lyle Berman, 3-time WSOP gold bracelet winner, founder of the World Poker Tour, and super-high stakes cash player; Bobby Baldwin, 1978 World Champion; Johnny Chan, 2-time World Champion and 10-time WSOP bracelet winner; Mike Caro, poker's greatest researcher, theorist, and instructor; Jennifer Harman, the world's top female player and one of ten best overall; Todd Brunson, winner of more than 20 tournaments; and Crandell Addington, no-limit hold'em legend. 704 pgs, $29.95.

CARO'S GUIDE TO DOYLE BRUNSON'S SUPER SYSTEM *by Mike Caro*. Working with World Champion Doyle Brunson, the legendary Mike Caro has created a fresh look to the "Bible" of all poker books, adding new and personal insights that help you understand the original work. Caro breaks 36 concepts into either "Analysis, Commentary, Concept, Mission, Play-By-Play, Psychology, Statistics, Story, or Strategy. Lots of illustrations and winning concepts give even more value to this great work. 86 pages, 8 1/2 x 11, $19.95.

ACCORDING TO DOYLE *by Doyle Brunson*. Learn what it takes to be a great poker player by climbing inside the mind of poker's most famous champion. Fascinating anecdotes and adventures from Doyle's early career playing poker in roadhouses are interspersed with lessons from the champion who has made more money at poker than anyone else in history. Learn what makes a great player tick, how he approaches the game, and receive candid, powerful advice from the legend himself. 208 pages, $14.95.

MY 50 MOST MEMORABLE HANDS *by Doyle Brunson*. This instant classic relives the most incredible hands by the greatest poker player of all time. Great players, legends, and poker's most momentous events march in and out of fifty years of unforgettable hands. Sit side-by-side with Doyle as he replays the excitement and life-changing moments of the most thrilling and crucial hands in the history of poker: from his early games as a rounder in the rough-and-tumble "Wild West" years—where a man was more likely to get shot as he was to get a straight flush—to the nail-biting excitement of his two world championship titles. Relive million dollar hands and the high stakes tension of sidestepping police, hijackers and murderers. A thrilling collection of stories and sage poker advice. 168 pages, $14.95.

THE GODFATHER OF POKER *by Doyle Brunson*. Doyle Brunson's riveting autobiography is a story of guts and glory, of good luck and bad, of triumph and unspeakable tragedy. It is a story of beating the odds, of a man who bet $1 million on a hole of golf—when he could barely stand! A master of the bluff, here is a man whose most outrageous bluff came with a gunman pointing a pistol at his forehead. He has survived whippings, gun fights, stabbings, mobsters, killers and a bout with cancer where the doctor told him his hand was played out. Apparently, fate had never played poker with Brunson; he lived. Doyle has searched for Noah's ark, tried to raise the Titanic, and won two poker championships. A must read. 352 pages, $26.95

THE CHAMPIONSHIP SERIES
POWERFUL INFORMATION YOU <u>MUST</u> HAVE

CHAMPIONSHIP NO-LIMIT & POT-LIMIT HOLD'EM *by T. J. Cloutier & Tom McEvoy.* New edition! The bible for winning pot-limit and no-limit hold'em gives you the answers to your most important questions: How do you get inside your opponents' heads and learn how to beat them at their own game? How can you tell how much to bet, raise, and reraise in no-limit hold'em? When can you bluff? How do you set up your opponents in pot-limit hold'em so that you can win a monster pot? What are the best strategies for winning no-limit and pot-limit tournaments, satellites, and supersatellites? Rock-solid and inspired advice you can bank on from two of the most recognizable figures in poker. 304 pages, $19.95.

CHAMPIONSHIP HOLD'EM *by T. J. Cloutier & Tom McEvoy.* New edition! Hard-hitting hold'em the way it's played *today* in both limit cash games and tournaments. Get killer advice on how to win more money in rammin'-jammin' games, kill-pot, jackpot, shorthanded, and full table cash games. You'll learn the thinking process for preflop, flop, turn, and river play with specific suggestions for what to do when good or bad things happen. Includes play-by-play analyses, advice on how to maximize profits against rocks in tight games, weaklings in loose games, experts in solid games, plus tournament strategies for small buy-in, big buy-in, rebuy, satellite and big-field major tournaments. Wow! 392 pages, $19.95.

CHAMPIONSHIP OMAHA (Omaha High-Low, Pot-limit Omaha, Limit High Omaha) *by Tom McEvoy & T.J. Cloutier.* New edition! Clearly-written strategies and powerful advice from Cloutier and McEvoy who have won four World Series of Poker Omaha titles. You'll learn how to beat low-limit and high-stakes games, play against loose and tight opponents, and the differing strategies for rebuy and freezeout tournaments. Learn the best starting hands, when slowplaying a big hand is dangerous, what danglers are (and why winners don't play them), why you sometimes fold the nuts on the flop and would be correct in doing so, and overall, how you can win a lot of money at Omaha! 272 pages, illustrations, $19.95.

CHAMPIONSHIP 107 HOLD'EM TOURNAMENT HANDS *by T. J. Cloutier & Tom McEvoy.* An absolute must for hold'em tournament players, two legends show you how to become a winning tournament player at both limit and no-limit hold'em games. Get inside the authors' heads as they think their way through the correct strategy at limit and no-limit starting hands. Cloutier & McEvoy show you how to use skill and intuition to play strategic hands for maximum profit in real tournament scenarios and how key hands were played by champions in turnaround situations at the WSOP. Gain tremendous insights into how tournament poker is played at the highest levels. 352 pages, $19.95.

CHAMPIONSHIP 7 STUD (Seven-Card Stud, Stud 8 or Better, and Razz) by Dr. Max Stern, Linda Johnson, and Tom McEvoy. 2011 New Edition! The authors, who have earned millions of dollars in major tournaments and cash games, eight World Series of Poker bracelets and hundreds of other titles in competition against the best players in the world show you the winning strategies for medium-limit side games as well as poker tournaments and a general tournament strategy that is applicable to any form of poker. Includes give-and-take conversations between the authors to give you more than one point of view on how to play poker. 224 pages, hand pictorials, photos. $19.95.

HOW TO WIN THE CHAMPIONSHIP: Hold'em Strategies for the Final Table, *by T.J. Cloutier.* T.J. Cloutier, the greatest tournament poker player ever—he has won 60 major tournament titles and appeared at 39 final tables at the WSOP, both more than any other player in the history of poker—shows how to get to the final table where the big money is made and then how to win it all. You'll learn how to build up enough chips to make it through the early and middle rounds and then how to employ T.J.'s own strategies to outmaneuver opponents at the final table and win championships. You'll learn how to adjust your play depending upon stack sizes, antes/blinds, table position, opponents styles, chip counts, and the specific strategies for six-handed, three handed, and heads-up play. 288 pages, $29.95.

POWERFUL WINNING POKER SIMULATIONS
A MUST FOR SERIOUS PLAYERS WITH A COMPUTER!
IBM compatible CD ROM Win 95, 98, 2000, NT, ME, XP

These incredible full color poker simulations are the best method to improve your game. Computer opponents play like real players. All games let you set the limits and rake and have fully programmable players, plus stat tracking, and Hand Analyzer for starting hands. Mike Caro, the world's foremost poker theoretician says, "Amazing... a steal for under $500... get it, it's great." Includes free phone support. "Smart Advisor" gives expert advice for every play!

1. TURBO TEXAS HOLD'EM FOR WINDOWS - $59.95. Choose which players, and how many (2-10) you want to play, create loose/tight games, and control check-raising, bluffing, position, sensitivity to pot odds, and more! Also, instant replay, pop-up odds, Professional Advisor keeps track of play statistics. Free bonus: Hold'em Hand Analyzer analyzes all 169 pocket hands in detail and their win rates under any conditions you set. Caro says this "hold'em software is the most powerful ever created." Great product!

2. TURBO SEVEN-CARD STUD FOR WINDOWS - $59.95. Create any conditions of play; choose number of players (2-8), bet amounts, fixed or spread limit, bring-in method, tight/loose conditions, position, reaction to board, number of dead cards, and stack deck to create special conditions. Features instant replay. Terrific stat reporting includes analysis of starting cards, 3-D bar charts, and graphs. Play interactively and run high speed simulation to test strategies. Hand Analyzer analyzes starting hands in detail. Wow!

3. TURBO OMAHA HIGH-LOW SPLIT FOR WINDOWS - $59.95. Specify any playing conditions; betting limits, number of raises, blind structures, button position, aggressiveness/passiveness of opponents, number of players (2-10), types of hands dealt, blinds, position, board reaction, and specify flop, turn, and river cards! Choose opponents and use provided point count or create your own. Statistical reporting, instant replay, pop-up odds high speed simulation to test strategies, amazing Hand Analyzer, and much more!

4. TURBO OMAHA HIGH FOR WINDOWS - $59.95. Same features as above, but tailored for Omaha High only. Caro says program is "an electrifying research tool...it can clearly be worth thousands of dollars to any serious player. A must for Omaha High players.

5. TURBO 7 STUD 8 OR BETTER - $59.95. Brand new with all the features you expect from the Wilson Turbo products: the latest artificial intelligence, instant advice and exact odds, play versus 2-7 opponents, enhanced data charts that can be exported or printed, the ability to fold out of turn and immediately go to the next hand, ability to peek at opponents hand, optional warning mode that warns you if a play disagrees with the advisor, and automatic mode that runs up to 50 tests unattended. Tough computer players vary their styles for a great game.

---

6. TOURNAMENT TEXAS HOLD'EM - $39.95

Set-up for tournament practice and play, this realistic simulation pits you against celebrity look-alikes. Tons of options let you control tournament size with 10 to 300 entrants, select limits, ante, rake, blind structures, freezeouts, number of rebuys and competition level of opponents. Pop-up status report shows how you're doing vs. the competition. Save tournaments in progress to play again later. Additional feature allows quick folds on finished hands.

Order now at 1-800-577-WINS or go online to: www.cardozabooks.com